ELIAS AL-MAQDISI & SAM SOLOMON

AL-YAHUD:

Eternal Islamic Enmity and the Jews

ANM
publishers

AL-yahuд:

Islamic Enmity and the Jews

BY ELIAS AL-MAQDISI & SAM SOLOMON

ISBN: 978-0-9715346-3-6 Paperback

Published by:

ANM
publishers

Advancing Native Missions
P.O. Box 5303
Charlottesville, VA 22905
www.Adnamis.org

ÐEÐICATION

To Elias Al-Maqdisi, my most beloved friend, most precious brother, and invaluable collaborator on many works pending and published.

Though born in Cairo, you lived almost all your life in Israel your beloved land, and in Jerusalem, your beloved city, so much so, that you became known among your colleagues and associates as "Al Maqdisi, The Jerusalemite, from Al-Quds" i.e., from Jerusalem.

Jerusalem, the most glorious city...the pearl of the whole world...the city of King David, Solomon, and Jesus...for whom you suffered so much, and so willingly.

I salute you my brother. And against all odds I will continue to uphold your mantle on your behalf, and for Him, whom your soul loved so much, and for the Jewish people.

I salute as well our other brothers and sisters, who have already come out of Islam, and those in substantial numbers who are coming to the realization that they must seek truth elsewhere, and are using their newfound platforms to warn others. To those of you, it is my hope that this book will provide the light needed to help you on your journey.

But first and foremost, this effort is ultimately dedicated to every Jew who has suffered from the legacy of Islamic enmity toward their people—starting from the Arabia of the 7th Century...till today...till the end of time. And for what...? For simply being a Jew.

And, no dedication of a book on this topic would be complete without giving mention and honour to the esteemed Professor Bat Ye'or whose landmark body of scholarship from 1974 to the present explains and documents the roots and reality of the legacy of the Islam of which I speak and whose prescient insights into the issues predated and predicted the resurgence we see before us.

I dedicate this book as well to my noble friend Professor Ariel Eldad, Member of the Knesset, for his tireless humane services to the people and the State of Israel—and to his courage and foresight.

And finally, I dedicate this work to the esteemed State of Israel itself, that great beacon of light which stands as a sentinel in the midst of the darkness, and steadfastly serves the rest of us like the canary in the mine-shaft—in facing the brunt of the 21st Century resurgence of Islam.

Sam Solomon

Acknowledgments

Elias and I started the writing of this book together, researched it, worked at it, shaped it, and brought it into draft form together. It is with great sadness and a heavy heart that I pen my thoughts at this time, as I approach the final fruition of our combined labours. It was his deepest desire to have seen this book out in his lifetime—nevertheless when it was obvious to him that his days were numbered on this earth he requested that it would be the first amongst a number of other works in the queue—as Jerusalem was his home and his passion.

Thus, with his desire uppermost in my mind, this particular book has been one of the most difficult tasks for me to contemplate and bring to completion following his departure last summer. Were it not for the enabling grace of the Lord I would not have been able to do it.

Uncountable and many worthwhile efforts over the centuries have preceded me, and here I would want to acknowledge them all with a "huge" thank you note for their contribution—so my thanks to the thousands of unnamed scholars, individuals and institutions. To name but a few ranging from individuals, to institutions—from Al Kindi to Raymond Lul to S. Zwemer, Bat Ye'or, D.L. Green, David Littman, Father Zakariya Butrous to Patrick Sookhdeo, Robert Spencer, Andrew Bostom and all others who have laboured and continue to labour exposing the myth of Islam as a "Religion of Peace."

An inexpressible thanks to all the esteemed institutions who labour so hard to keep us updated from Answering Islam to MEMRI and all those worthy websites.

Amongst this worthy cloud of witnesses, I would want to mention Wafa Sultan for her boldness and Mus'ab Hassan Yousef, son of Hamas's leader, who against all the odds and a grievous risk to his life has publicly declared his newly found faith in Christ and his love for his old enemies "the Jews".

My most sincere thanks to all those others who have read, edited, type-set, and enthusiastically provided all sorts of things. Most importantly my inexpressible gratitude to those who have prayed and continue to pray so that this humble work might be effectively used in dispelling the myths, misinformation, and exceedingly potent disinformation that surrounds one of the most critical topics of our times, none other than "Al-Yahud: The Jews and the Islamic doctrine of enmity towards them".

Sam Solomon

CONTENTS

why this book is needed!

One might say, what can one more book on this subject do to unlock the historic roots of the conflict/enmity between the Muslims and the Jews? And what difference would it make anyway, as world leaders have already decided to join together to step in and bring "peace" to the Middle East by imposing a Two-State solution? To this end, well meaning people with an understandable motivation to find peace at any cost theorize hopefully, *"No matter how the problem got started, the solution remains the same. What we need is a proper allocation of the land to the Palestinian Arabs and a resolution of their competing desire for social justice and political identity."*

This is the currently popular humanistic expression of the conflict which is the basis and framework for the worldwide outcry for resolution—after several generations of support for Israel by the USA, Canada and European powers. The idea here is that if this pragmatic framing of the conflict is true—even Israel herself will benefit from a cessation of hostilities by once more giving land for peace, thus putting (what is seen by outsiders) as a proper final solution to the age-old conflict.

But what if the Islamic counter-claims to the land are only a smoke-screen emanating from, and obscuring several earlier and more important key decisions regarding the Jewish presence and Islamic claims to the "land" and Monotheism—as taken in the 7th century by Muhammad personally, during the formative days of Islam, and thus long before any Muslim either saw or set foot on the Holy Land?

What could those key decisions be? And, how could these key decisions by one man cast the die which would seal the eternal fate of Jewish-Muslim relations as well as the fate of Jerusalem and the entire Holy Land? On the bottom line, is this conflict with modern Israel really a limited political/ethnic Palestinian issue over the "land" and "social justice" set in the 19th through the 21st centuries, or is it a basic and eternal Islamic issue of "enmity" as proclaimed, and mandated toward the Jews—both as individuals and collectively—from within the pages of the Qur'an and the Sunnah of Muhammad?

That's the heart of this book.

As referred to above, current humanist writers, Islamist leaders, and Palestinian spokespeople from the Muslim and Christian perspectives are presenting the case that the root of bitterness, or "enmity" between the current Palestinian factions and Israel has been caused by generations of strife and conflict primarily over the land since Jews began what is termed the "return", which resulted in the displacement of the Palestinians—and can thus only be ameliorated by "helping" the parties to take steps toward a Two-State solution.

Hence , we maintain that in the thinking behind this Two-State solution, the "results" and the "reasons" are being reversed, such that the "results" of strife over the "land"—the continuing strife and human suffering on both sides—are being cast as the root "reasons" for the conflict instead of the other way around.

An analogy which would encapsulate this fallacious framing of the conflict would be the example that "fever" is the "result", not the "cause" of an underlying infection—so that in treating the fever alone, or in this case the analogous "land" issue as the sole reason for the conflict, one will only rid oneself of the warning signs while leaving the root causes intact.

In so doing, what progress would be made toward world peace in the long run by enforcing a type of truce, or temporary "peace" through a Two-State solution that would leave the root issues of the Qur'anic mandates toward severe treatment of the Jews intact?

Furthermore, and quite ironically, now that this prospect of a political solution through the creation of two states side by side is looking more and more popular and thus apparently more enforceable by the international community, the Palestinians and the various Muslim nations who earlier voiced enthusiastic support of this compromise plan are getting over-confident and are now calling for even more—including the possible demand of sole ownership of Jerusalem as the Palestinian capital—based not simply on ethnic Palestinian rights to Jerusalem as their capital (over the historic rights of Jewish and Christian Jerusalemites), but on overriding eternal Islamic claims to the land as a doctrinal "Waqf[1]", which would nullify any prior Jewish or Christian rights or claims.

Now this raises another issue, which we will deal with as well—and that is, where did the Islamic doctrinal claim to Jerusalem come from, and why is this being portrayed in the media and in the "negotiations" as a Palestinian issue rather than the non-augmentable Islamic issue that it is?

However, to recap and summarize, this is just to establish that the most prevalent public and diplomatic opinion today is that the issue preventing resolution is primarily that of political and humanitarian conflicts over the "land," and resultant enmity coming from decades of struggles over the land. This makes a certain logic, but suffers from the lack of knowledge and understanding of the Islamic source books, as well as the firm grip that the Qur'an has on the everyday life of Muslims—and how as a consequence, all that is in the Qur'an and the Sunnah shape today's applications of prescribed enmity of Muslims towards the Jews and the 'other'. So, if this is true, one must ask—"What is really in the Qur'an about the Jews?

In this book we will lay out these doctrines, how they came about, how they are applied and how they explain once and for all the Islamic "enmity" toward the Jews that has been seen down through the centuries, and how the Islamic political and religious counterclaims can be understood within that context as thinly veiled attempts to justify this "enmity", and to lay further claim to Jewish lands, traditions, and perhaps shockingly—even the origin of Judeo-Christian Monotheism itself. Note that each of these Qur'anic doctrines is fully documented in the extensive appendix, including contemporary affirmations by Islamic authorities contained in recent public statements and official rulings given in Fatwas.

Having exposed the source of this "enmity", and it's expression at the points of greatest offense to Islam in the founding of Israel and in the later

---

[1] Please see full explanations of this term and its Islamic understanding in Chapter 6.

reclaiming of Jerusalem—we will show how it is the enmity itself that fuels and drives "Jihad" in all of its forms—toward the Jew first but ultimately to all religions, as when it comes to Jihad, no non-Muslim is exempt.

In short—this book relates to one basic but emerging theme: The 7th century origins of Islamic enmity to the Jews commencing with Muhammad's announcement of his mission to correct and complete the Jewish and Christian revelations, and thus in his eyes, "restore" Islamic Monotheism—with its continuing implications to the current Arab-Israeli conflict in the Middle East, and beyond to the wider global context.

The Authors

PREFACE
And...what this book is not about!

Clearly, with the above in mind, we will not be engaging in a blow by blow account of the contemporary permutations of the various and inevitable "results" stemming from the root issues of original 7th century Islamic "enmity" which have the effect of displacing "cause" with "effect" so that the "results" are all too often seen by outsiders as framing the problem itself.

We maintain that the source of these apparently unending cycles of violence can be literally laid within the Islamic source documents, and the continuing affirmations made by the Islamic authorities and leaders of each generation who function so as to keep the Muslim society on track to express and enforce Qur'anically mandated enmity toward the Jews—and thus to Israel.

Therefore do not expect a running account of the complex issues which are currently percolating within the political give and take between the Palestinians and Israel—such as the stages of the delicate "negotiations" or platforms presented by both sides such as the meetings in Madrid, Oslo, Cairo, Rome, Brussels and Camp David to mention a few.

In fact, there are libraries full of such writings, and it is these which have contributed to the covering over of the root issues we are bringing to light, which in turn and in due time have produced political and humanitarian violations—which themselves have been substituted as the "problem" itself, rather than the "result" of a long-standing prescribed Islamic enmity toward the Jews long before modern Israel was ever thought of. Such jockeying for advantage and subsequent speculative writings obscure the fullness and depth of the conflict and thus prevent the formulation of a valid framework for resolution of the conflict based on solid and provable root issues.

Therefore, this book does not give any proposed political solutions or accounts of delicate negotiations.

Instead, the only mention of the political and social factors we will make will be in order to set the proper historical and circumstantial context for the key issues to be discussed and brought into focus.

Another topic that this is book is NOT about—at any great length—is the extended complexities of the Muslim relationships to the Christians or to the "Other" (i.e. adherents of other religions), except in establishing the dynamics and basic parameters of the Islamic collective attitude toward the Jews and Christians as the "People of the Book", while presenting some cursory implications to those religions which are outside this allegedly "protected" zone of worshippers.

Hence, we shall maintain our focus on the original and lasting Islamic position on the key issue of what the Qur'an and the Sunnah say about the Jews, and the related land issues—documenting each major point, chapter and verse, in the substantial appendix.

Thus, we shall show that the Qur'anic account of the Jews as "People of the Book" with a sharply curtailed and subservient role in regard to the bringing of Monotheism is but a brief interlude during which time mention of their original elevation as the "custodians" of the Islamic revelations through Abraham and the other Patriarchs is noted, but is soon abrogated and descends rapidly to the level of charges and penalties as to how, from Allah's perspective, they fell from grace to condemnation, and having had their favoured status with Allah "revoked", they have now forfeited any claims or rights before mankind.

This written account of their limited and brief role and subsequent demotion in the pages of the Qur'an is graphic, and is quite substantial. As you will see, pre-occupation with the Jews takes up more than 60% of the entire text—not including the substantial affirmations and extensions of the expressed "enmity" within the Sunnah of Muhammad (his words, acts and what he consented to), so that the discrediting and disenfranchisement of the Jews can be seen to emanate from the highest levels of Islam, coming directly and concurrently from Allah and his messenger Muhammad.

This brings us to one last topic which this book is NOT about. Though we will show that the root of enmity toward the Jews fuels the attitudes of Muslims toward them wherever they may live and especially in response to Israel—and thus is a main factor in the Islamic Jihad against the Jews—we will NOT go into the fine details of the various types and names of Jihad. But we will instead limit ourselves to the source of the enmity that drives and justifies Jihad in all its forms.

Thus we will present the case that given the original and lasting Islamic pronouncements within the Islamic sources regarding the Jews—the current so-called Arab-Israeli conflict must be framed within this wider context in order to be able to make any sense of it, or to propose any solutions which would hope to be lasting.

Basically…we are positing our approach on the Einsteinian premise—that any problem has to be defined and framed correctly before a solution can be formulated, much less presented—as the guiding principle of this treatise.

We firmly maintain that the solution is always in the analysis of the problem…leaving you with the fearful caveat, "Whoever has ears to hear, let him hear…"

CHAPTER 1
Setting the Context: The Search for the Bottom Line

Climate of enmity

The existence of the "Doctrine of Enmity" in Islam can be sensed in events and attitudes towards Christians and Jews today and throughout history—engendering a "climate" of enmity. This climate is evidenced in those widespread and visibly hostile attitudes, seen and read about daily but which are obscured by Islamic claims to the contrary, to be a religion of peace, and one that respects all of the Judeo-Christian prophets, as well as other religions.

Yet this very palpable climate is not dispelled by such apologetics, but instead remains in one's memory as an evidence, or undercurrent—and for good reason. Sometimes one can feel or sense a danger which one cannot prove at the time—but that doesn't mean it isn't there, as it could just be hidden from view.

This is surely the case with enmity in Islam—as Muhammad has veiled this doctrine and embedded it within a web of complementary doctrines and apparently benign terminologies so that not all comprehend its existence, much less its depth and breadth. We will show that though unseen by the un-initiated, it is definitely there—and constitutes a complex framework for identifying and defining enmity, then applying it and enforcing it, on the Jews first, then the Christians, and at last on all non-Muslim mankind.

We have asked the question, "But why?" This will become clear as we establish the development of the rationale which would emerge to become a formal doctrine given by Allah during the early days of Islam, and as such, both absolute and enforceable for eternity.

This will be accomplished by starting with some few instances wherein one can see and feel the looming but invisible presence of such a doctrine in the attitudes expressed toward the Jews (and Christians), in the Qur'an and the Sunnah, as well as attitudes which are expressed toward the State of Israel.

Manifestations of the enmity doctrine & the Jews
Jews and Christians in the Muslim daily prayers

Every day a modest estimate of at least hundreds of millions of Muslims the world over align themselves in the direction of Mecca, Saudi Arabia where the cubic building called the Ka'aba is situated to pray and worship. But what do they pray? It might shock you to know exactly what they pray in the name of Allah the most high.

In each of the five daily ritual prayers, they pray the opening Sura[2] of the Qur'an ending in the two verses, *"Guide us to the straight path, the path of those whom You have favoured with guidance, not [the path] of those against whom there is wrath, nor of those who are astray."* [Sura 1:6-7]

In the interpretation of the last verse, Muslim scholars are in unanimous agreement that *"those against whom there is wrath"* are

---

What do Muslims pray 5 times daily in the name of Allah, the most high?

Is the prayer recited at dawn, noon, afternoon, sunset and evening by hundreds of millions of Muslims a blessing or a curse?

In each of the five daily ritual prayers, Muslims around the world pray the opening Sura of the Qur'an ending in these two verses, *"Guide us to the straight path, the path of those whom You have favoured with guidance, not [the path] of those against whom there is wrath, nor of those who are astray."* [Sura 1:6-7]... Muslim scholars are in unanimous agreement that *"those against whom there is wrath"* are the Jews...While *"those who are astray"* are identified as being the Christians.

---

the Jews[3], who have incurred Allah's wrath, for though having allegedly received the scriptures and the revelations of the coming prophet, who is the seal of all prophets, namely Muhammad, it is stated in the Qur'an that they concealed this revelation—hence justly incurring the divine and eternal wrath of Allah. While *"those who are astray"* are identified as being the Christians[4], who have blasphemed by adding "partners" to Allah.

Though these Qur'anic verses in the opening Sura are in "code" recognizable only by its adherents, in essence this is a concealed but implicit castigation and condemnation of Jews and Christians embedded within the formal daily prayers of all Muslims.

Therefore, when one multiplies this prayer times five times a day, for 1.4 billion Muslims worldwide, this is a sobering thought indeed. Especially when one realizes that these condemnations as referenced in the Qur'an are coming directly from Allah—and therefore carry both temporal and eternal penalties.

For emphasis, let us recap that what we have seen here is essentially "curses" imbedded in the key ritual prayer which is being uttered five times a day in every country where there is a practicing Muslim—whether he be nominal, moderate, or fundamentalist. That too is a sobering thought.

Furthermore, the historical implications are staggering, as Muslims have been reciting that Sura, and thus in effect, cursing the Jews and Christians in a type of "code" at least since January, 624 A.D., the second year of the Hijra, (immigration of Muhammad from Mecca to Medina), without (subsequent generations) being fully cognizant of what was meant by these veiled references.

Early glimmers

However, the Jews living in Medina, which at the time of the Hijrah was a Jewish city known as Yathrib—became very aware of these

---

[2] Exclusive divine name reserved for a "chapter" of the Qur'an.

[3] See for example *Arab Theologians on Jews and Israel*, D.L. Green ed.; Ed. De l'Avenir, Geneva (1976). ASIN: B000I90TBO.

[4] http://www.altafsir.com/Tafasir.asp?tMadhNo=1&tTafsirNo=74&tSoraNo=1&tAyahNo=7&tDisplay=yes&UserProfile=0&LanguageId=2

nuances during the brief "honeymoon" period in which Muhammad tried to win them over.

For example, for 17 months after the immigration, Muslims at that time were praying in the direction of Jerusalem. Other apparent concessions were also made, such as the introduction of a "fast" modeled on the Jewish fast as a central Islamic ritual— and the inclusion in the Qur'an of the names (without the corresponding Jewish "identities") of all the major Jewish patriarchs such as Abraham, Moses, Joseph, etc, giving the distinct impression to the Jews of the time that Muhammad's new religion was perhaps compatible with Judaism, and certainly not a threat, even if it had already been seen to be contradictory in issues such as Muhammad's prophethood as being the fulfillment of the Jewish prophecies.

Clearly they had the scriptures to disprove his claim to fulfill their prophecies, so that as they became more conversant with his claims, their jokes at his expense were a major factor in Muhammad's growing enmity towards them.

The inexplicable and veiled nature of these glimmers

However, all during the same period of time that Muhammad was courting their favor, these veiled "curses" were ringing out undetected as such through their streets and markets without the true meaning ever being understood as being carefully constructed covert curses, much less as curses which would apply to them. So it can be seen that the "enmity" to them was already there in covert form within the daily prayers of the first community of Muslims, even before the Jews began to expose the errors in Muhammad's claims. To this day, the same phenomenon as happened in Medina so long ago, is happening daily to Jews and Christians through-out the Muslim and non-Muslim countries to the extent that increasingly popular Muslim-Jewish and Muslim-Christian "Interfaith Dialogue" activities proceed without either the Christians or the Jews realizing that they, like the Jews of Medina before them, are being lavishly courted through polite and erudite dialogue and fellowship— all the while they are being "cursed" and condemned by their hosts through the "coded" daily prayers, and much more.

"Tolerance?" But the enmity is eternal!

This level of prescribed divine "enmity" that lasts unabated through the centuries down to today without any reprieve or chance of reprieve may be shocking and rather difficult to believe at first—since it is well known that Jews and Christians are granted an apparent form of tolerance as "People of the Book". The status of "People of the Book" is thought to be a privileged and "safe" position within Islamic states with rights to worship, but in actuality, it is just the opposite, and is instead a state of virtual bondage with severe legal limitations, boundaries, and penalties.

But even that is not the full extent of it.

In addition to these illustrated condemnations and "curses" in the daily prayers, the Qur'anic injunctions include a divinely mandated requirement or "doctrine" for Muslims to maintain a level of socially expressed "enmity", or "prescribed separation" toward both Christians and Jews—except in a case such as Interfaith Dialogue as just mentioned, or other pragmatic circumstances wherein it is necessary for a Muslim, or the Muslim community itself to be in relationship with non-Muslims for the benefit and furtherance of the cause of Islam. We are seeing this doctrine of "separation," or self-imposed segregation in full gear in the Muslim communities within host countries of the Western world today especially in Europe and the UK.

However, the case of enmity toward the Jews is a special case. It is foundational and more extreme in the Islamic framework of the doctrine of enmity, and is much more an expression with an imperative to action than is the prescribed Christian enmity, and hence has become front page news, because it is reflected daily in the ongoing Arab-Israeli conflict.

Muslim–Jewish crisis as perceived in current public opinion

Is there an unseen agenda?

Recently there have been attempts by the defenders and propagators of Islam, as well as some Arab and Muslim politicians, to downplay the depth of the so-called Arab-Israeli conflict by presenting it purely as a salvable political crisis rather than face the full implications of the obvious moral and religious issues which are at the heart of the crisis—by simply leaving out the crucial fact that Islam is both political and religious. Their argument blatantly ignores the obvious predilection toward "enmity" to the Jews within Islamic sources, and asserts that this conflict will end, as soon as, the political and economical injustices imposed by Israel on the Palestinian Arabs are addressed and resolved by the establishment of

> **When addressing the Arab-Israeli conflict, which agenda is it?**
>
> Since Islam itself is both political and religious, the political/pragmatic rationale and the religious/Islamic rationale both lend themselves for use by all perspectives in making their arguments, and are used alternatively—often in the same conversation—to create a type of circular reasoning. This characteristic method of alternating between the two, is a major technique in the smokescreen response to each and every issue of this complex conflict.

a proper Palestinian state side by side with a Hebrew or an Israeli state. This characteristic alternating between the political and religious is a major factor in the smokescreen response to each and every issue of the conflict as will be discussed in more detail in Chapter 2.

Other stakeholders: There are many Arab Jews (and Christians)

However before we proceed any further, let's make it clear that generally most people equate Arabs with Muslims, forgetting that there are at least 14 Million Arab Christians in the Arab world. What may come as surprise is that there are significant numbers of Arab Jews as well. Historically, according to Acts of Apostles in the New Testament Bible and the distinguished historian Josephus the proselytised Jews and normal Jews as according to their practice had come to Jerusalem to celebrate a Jewish festival (Feast of Pentecost). They were from Libya, Arabia, Persia, etc. That means that the Jews were not just one ethnic group but they were from all nations. In the Arab world, there were many Arabs who had embraced Judaism. Following the advent of Christ, many of these Arab Jews had embraced the Christian faith…as well as many pagan Arabs who had embraced Christianity. "Arab" used to mean only those who were in the region of Yemen and the greater Arabian Peninsula.

Because of the coming of Islam and Islamic conquest all others such as the Arabian nomads, and the tribes of Iraq, Syria, the Egyptian Copts, the North Africans, and others were Islamized and Arabized – hence the region was transformed from being Judeo-Christian to Arabized Islam. Nevertheless, many of the Christians and Jews survived, though humiliated and subdued, they still survived…Even today there are at least over 4,000 Jewish families in Syria as original Arab Syrians. Likewise those Jews expelled from Egypt in 1956 by Nasser were all Egyptian Jews who had been there for generations. These Jews were not European Jews who had immigrated…a commonly held misconception. There are Indian Jews in India, a large constituency, even today. Also there are African Jews who were transported through the Sudan from Ethiopia[5] (known as the Falasha Jews). In Iran there used to be a thriving Jewish community until recently, who trace their heritage back to Babylonian days, but now there are a very few. For instance the Moroccan and North African Jewish communities are well traced by Bat Ye'or in her book "The Dhimmis: Jews and Christians under Islam."

It is to be noted that as modern-day Islamization is progressing swiftly in the Arab and non-Arab but Muslim countries, the Jewish and Christian communities there are being threatened and are dwindling in numbers.

The "Two-State solution" contingent

Back to the subject of the conflict, as earlier stated, most political leaders in the West, the Arab Countries, Russia, China, most UN members and even the Palestinian Authority, are convinced that the "Two-State solution" is the only viable alternative to lasting peace between Israel and its neighbours. One such example is a recent article by former U.S. president Jimmy Carter published in October, 2009, in the Washington Post entitled, "The Elders' View of the Middle East".[6] He states in his conclusion, "A Two-State solution is clearly preferable and has been embraced at the grass roots."

---

[5] http://www.falasha-recordings.co.uk/teachings/ras.html

[6] http://www.washingtonpost.com/wp-dyn/content/article/2009/09/04/AR2009090402968.html

Theoretically, and logically—without the benefit of the knowledge of the Qur'anic mandates—former President Carter would have a point. From the political and human points of view the Arab-Israeli conflict is neither unique, nor is it of such a huge dimension that it could not be resolved with compromises on all sides. Like many other conflicts in the world and throughout history, such population shifts though traumatic were eventually resolved to greater or lesser degrees, and did not fester indefinitely. For example, even in the Middle East itself, and before the establishment of Israel in 1948, the Republic of Turkey under Ataturk carried out the annexation of the Aleksandretta (or Hatay) province in Northwest Syria and the forced emigration of the majority of its Arab population[7]. In spite of this, the relations between Syria and Turkey have been normalized and today they both cooperate in many areas. Actually, the numbers of affected Syrian-Arab people is comparable to the Palestinian refugees of the 1948 war in Palestine.

So, why is the Arab-Israeli conflict still festering?

Alternating between the "political" and the "religious"

There are manifold reasons in this complex situation, most of which we will touch upon—but the manipulation of the "political" vs the "religious" is employed in all of them.

Our premise is that the "political" is only one aspect of a wide ranging set of deeper issues from the pages of Islamic sources which must be explored before a viable and lasting solution could be considered. Keeping in mind that since the curses in regard to the Jews are hidden, or "veiled" within the coded references of the Qur'an, this leaves the Muslims free to quote the various Sura's, and alternate between the different nuances when challenged about their treatment of the Jews to hide the deeper and harsher condemnations from public view. Likewise, Muslims alternate between the established "religious/Islamic" doctrines and the "political/pragmatic" possibilities when speaking of the Arab-Israeli crisis also as a diversion or smokescreen, in order to obscure their true intent in regard to the "land" issues.

Thus, from a strategic perspective the Arab-Israeli conflict has given Islamists a major platform to advance the Islamic agenda almost simultaneously, while bolstering their own political position.[8] All of the coded rhetoric is accomplished without doing anything to actually alleviate the distress of the affected Palestinian refugees who themselves are supposed to be the crux of the problem.

In fact, these refugees depend more on non-Islamic and international donations than on Islamic ones. And those Palestinians who managed to start new lives in other parts of the world; they did so on their own and against large odds from their "Arab and Muslim brothers."

Palestinian "Diaspora" gives credence to a secular state

The role of the Palestinian secular/academic component

In approaching the reason as to "why" this crisis has simmered rather than being resolved as have other such large population shifts—one must consider the large numbers of Palestinians who have immigrated to Western Countries.

---

[7] According to the record, "Syrians hold the view that this land was illegally ceded to Turkey by France, the mandatory occupying power of Syria in the late 1930s. Syria still considers it an integral part of its own territory. Syrians call this land Liwa' aliskenderun (Arabic: لواء الاسكندرون) rather than the Turkish name of Hatay." (See http://en. wikipedia.org/wiki/Hatay_Province#Turkish-Syrian_dispute_over_the_Hatay_Province).

[8] See Arab Theologians on Jews and Israel 1968/ Introduced and edited by D.L. Green. Quoting from this reference, "Dr. Abdul Halim Mahmoud, then Head of the Islamic Research Academy and Rector of Al Azhar University, later published Jihad and Victory in which he made the same point about the Jews according to Scripture (i.e. The Qur'an): ...Allah commands the Muslims to fight the friends of Satan wherever they are found. Among the friends of Satan — indeed among the foremost friends of Satan in our age — are the Jews. The Jews have laid down a program for the destruction of humanity, through subverting religion and ethics. They have already begun their control of the mass media, and their propaganda. They have falsified knowledge, violated standards of literary truth, and put conscience in the service of breaking down to implement this programme with their money, and destroying humanity. As a consequence of such activities, the Jews have succeeded in gaining control and seizing power. But Allah...will wreck the edifice that the Jews have built and eliminate their destructive machinations and double-dealing."

> ## Palestinian academicians foster legitimacy for Palestinian rights
>
> Both contingents—those who want a political/pragmatic solution and those who want to adhere to the Islamic/religious rationale make extensive use of this new "intellectual legitimacy" of Palestine in the global

In considering this factor, one must not underestimate the effect of the substantial "Palestinian Diaspora", who in immigrating to the West in large numbers because of the difficulty presented by the refusal of Arab countries to welcome them as full citizens have effectively developed the "political" case for the "secular state of Palestine" as well as the case against Israel for allegedly making them the "victims"— while effectively presenting themselves as the witnesses and advocates for their case.

We will show how those Palestinians who became citizens in Western countries in particular have become a very influential and erudite force in presenting the Palestinian case from within academia, the media and Western "Think Tanks"—such that their influence is substantial on foreign policy no matter what country they now call home.

Some few selected examples would include such personalities as Palestinian Professors Edward Said (Christian) and Walid Al-Khalidi (Muslim), plus an untold numbers of lesser known but equally effective advocates of Palestinian agendas.

Unfortunately, many of these academicians engage in one form or another of what could be termed "the rewriting of history," or disinformation. Their writings span the spectrum from mild criticisms and/or corrections of the Israeli historic narrative to outright denial of the factual historicity of the Jewish archaeology. One mild example of this phenomenon is that of Shamekh Alawneh, a lecturer in modern history at Al-Quds Open University, who recently said on a television programme called Jerusalem - History and Culture that the Jews invented the connection to the Wailing Wall for political purposes, whereas this is but a fabrication for purposes of the "Judaization of Jerusalem."[9]

This is only the tip of the iceberg as substantial efforts are being made within Western universities to thoroughly deconstruct or discredit the Jewish archaeological record in support of Islamic claims to the Temple of

Solomon under cover of "Palestinian rights", including escalating claims for other landmarks throughout the Holy Land. This disinformation has gained validity within such notable universities as Columbia, Harvard, and others. There have been substantial protests from among the alumni of at least one of these universities on the basis that this is a transparent and obvious misuse of academia to advance a political agenda—but to little avail in the prevailing literary climate of similar refutations of history based on the fading but still virile "de-construction" principle. This prevailing so-called "academic license" thus both refutes Israeli claims, and provides a form of intellectual legitimacy for Palestinian claims—thus lifting the Palestinian banner for "liberation" from the grip of the "usurper".

Both contingents—those who want a political/pragmatic solution and those who want to adhere to the Islamic religious rationale make extensive use of this new "intellectual legitimacy" of Palestine in the global public consciousness.

"Liberating" Palestine...or "deconstructing" Israel?

The use of enmity toward Israel on the banner of "liberating Palestine" is not new, as it has been employed by the Arab states in very heavy handed ways since the first days of the Statehood of Israel. But what is new during the past decade or so, is this emerging apparent secular "legitimacy" for the Palestinian rights that has been carefully constructed in academia on the back of the deconstruction wave to cover over the reality of the underlying Islamic claims at the base of the "religious/Islamic" rationale. This apparent "legitimacy" is being used effectively and concurrently by a wide spectrum of political, military, and terrorist groups[10].

One contingent would include the West, all the Arab countries, as well as the Palestinian Authority (PA) who are in basic agreement in support of the so-called "Road Map" which is based on a Two-State solution—

---

[9] http://www.rightsidenews.com/200908226111/global-terrorism/no-jewish-connection-to-western-wall-pa-university-lecturer.html

[10] See D. L. Green, *Arab Theologians on Jews and Israel* based on the 1968 Forth Conference of the Academy of Islamic Research, Al Azhar University, Cairo, Egypt.

which they say would constitute the final settlement of the Arab-Israeli conflict. However, the West is oblivious to the undercurrent of support for the doctrinal "religious/Islamic" position which is regularly being given to the Muslim public with the tacit approval of these same Arab governments who are apparently supporting a political solution.

The other contingent would be those who are explicit about their dedication to the "religious/Islamic" rationale. As an illustration of this thinking, let us consider four examples:

- HAMAS (Ḥarakat al-Muqāwamat al-Islāmiyyah, meaning "Islamic Resistance Movement") has all along used the Islamic doctrines against the Jews (See 1988 "Hamas Covenant..." or constitution[11]) to assert their influence on the rest of the Palestinian population. This is evidenced by their unrelenting opposition to the Two-State solution both before and after Yasser Arafat concluded the Oslo agreement. Their subsequent winning of the elections to take over the control of Gaza has made their influence more widely known in the West.

- Hizbullah Party in Lebanon is also based on the doctrinal Qur'anic mandates against the Jews and Israel and has no tolerance for the political/pragmatic position. In so doing it has managed to build a major fighting force, used it to provoke the 2006 war with Israel, and then turned to deploy their newfound military capability domestically to exert control over the internal politics of the Lebanese Republic.

- On the other hand the Islamic Republic of Iran, that had no direct political conflict whatsoever with Israel (other than the internal Qur'anic mandate), has been the champion against Israel going as far as to develop nuclear weapons and to announce that the destruction of Israel is No. 1 on its agenda, and that the Jewish holocaust did not even take place. These excesses are prime examples of the application of the Islamic mandate in the Qur'an toward the Jews.

---

[11] See "The Covenant of the Islamic Resistance Movement." http://www.mideastweb.org/hamas.htm

This has allowed the Islamic radical sector of the contemporary Iranian society to maintain control of the country despite the large-scale opposition that was evident after the last elections. Contrast this with the regime of Shah Reza Pahlavi prior to the Islamic Revolution of 1979. At the time, Iran had a vibrant Jewish community and strong economic and political ties to Israel. In fact it was these ties that contributed to his overthrow by Islamic fundamentalists.

- And of course, the ultimate champions of the Qur'anic mandates, Bin-Laden and Al-Qaeda contingents, are adamant on the destruction of Israel as a starting point for many other well-known activities. In every clandestine video through channels such as Al-Jazeera TV, Bin Laden and Al-Zawaheri consistently blame the "Crusader-Zionist" conspiracy as the main cause of the weakness of the Arab and Islamic worlds.

In short, one will not be able to understand these complex and often counterintuitive developments unless the extent, reasons and nature and roots of the Islamic enmity to the Jews is identified, explained and properly understood. Only then will one have the context necessary to be able to address the results of that enmity as it plays out within the culture in conflicts over "land."

How central is "the land" in the dispute?

The Gordian knot

Again we ask, is it really true that the Arab-Israeli conflict is solely a political conflict over land—a conflict which emerged out of nowhere following centuries of supposed "compatible" Jewish/Muslim relations— a conflict that started with no warning signs with the Balfour Declaration and subsequent establishment of an Israeli state in 1948?

The current assumptions of well-meaning world leaders, who see the crisis over a Palestinian state as the Gordian knot which if cut, would cathartically satisfy the root issue behind the actions of a long list of Islamist terror organizations within and without the Palestinian territory— would reply with a resounding "yes" to both questions. In their reasoning, this interpretation frames the conflict, and thus provides the rationale for addressing a final solution which they theorize would result in an almost instant "peace" being brought to the Middle East and the whole world.

The basis of this assumption is that the Jews are "occupiers"[12] by nature, and thus as a habit have been known to have been usurpers of the lands of others, and therefore their political ambitions must be reined in by the international community.

In line with these assumptions and in support of the political model as the rationale for the current conflict, we would further ask, if this be true, then when and where were the historic examples of such previous "political conflicts" initiated by the Jews over "land" issues? As a matter of record, there were none, but quite the opposite—going back to the 7th century and the very beginning of Islam.

So, we repeat the obvious question: Is it true that the land is the major issue?[13]

Third parties can't see beyond the political "land" issues

To understand this from a non-stakeholder or third-party position (those who are not involved like Western governments) we need to see how the stakeholders themselves view or report it. These third parties, or non-participants, normally are trying their best to ascertain the facts as objectively as possible without realizing the tactics deployed by the Muslims to win the case. The case being, for the Muslims—it is not necessary to win the argument or to solve the problem, or settle the issue, but rather to serve a greater overarching cause, i.e. the "religious/Islamic" cause, which most of the time remains hidden or veiled.

Thus, to the outsider it is a pragmatic matter of solving the problem of the needy and deprived Palestinians. Whereas to the Palestinians and the Arab/Islamic world, the Palestinian-Israeli crisis is just the tip of the iceberg—with the iceberg being the greater Islamic agenda to implement the mandates of the Qur'an toward the Jews and the land.

Hence the desire is not to solve the problem, because by solving the problem the greater agenda within the Qur'an will be neutralized and therefore rendered ineffective. So the deployed tactic is to concentrate on the hot button issue of the land, capitalize on the world sympathy for the plight of the Palestinians, weave through the recognition of the "peaceful nature of Islam" and other building blocks of the Islamic argument. Therefore, in essence Islamic leaders see the Palestinian issue as a gateway issue to the greater goal.

Top Muslim authority plays the alternating theme

Muslims, when addressing the West on this issue have sought to justify this view that there is "no problem" with the "Jewishness" aspect, but only with the issue of the land.   One such recent attempt was the statement by Sheikh Yousef Al-Qaradawi[14], speaking to the Western audiences, *"the struggle between us and the Jews is over the land and not over their Jewishness."*

He continued, "For they are the ***People of the Book*** (our emphasis), we are allowed to eat their food and marry their women. Sura 5:5 states, *'Made lawful to you this day are foods, which Allah has made lawful. The food of the people of the Scripture (Jews and Christians) is lawful to you and yours is lawful to them. (Lawful to you in marriage) are chaste women from the believers and chaste women from those who were given the Scripture (Jews and Christians) before your time.'"* Aside from the logical inconsistency involving the approval to allow a Muslim man to marry a Christian or Jewish woman, but not vice versa—his statement would give the impression of full cultural and social acceptance.   But is that just a part of the smokescreen, and a prime example of the "coded" aspect? Indeed, it is.

---

[12] Arab theologians on Jews and Israel edited by D.F. Green

[13] Dr Kamel el Baker President of Omdurman Islamic University Sudan, Page 59 Arab Theologians on Jews and Israel/ DLGreen. Quoting Dr. el Baker, "…Zionism is the same as Judaism …the establishment of a Jewish state in Palestine means a confrontation of Islam and Muslims, for the cultural and demographic superiority in the usurped land is for Islam and Muslim…"

[14] Full text of Al-Qaradawi statement (in Arabic) http://www.bramjnet.com/vb3/showthread.php?t=245834

When addressing his Muslim constituency in the Arabic language, however, Al-Qaradawi reverses himself by issuing statements to the contrary on the same exact topic. Here is the statement whereby he is addressing a Muslim[15]audience about the Jews (The original is in Arabic and is given in the footnote):

"Jews are the greatest enemies of the Ummah (the worldwide Muslim community)! And their enmity to Islam and Muslims has been, still is and will continue as long as Muslims and Jews remain on this earth. This issue has been settled without question or argument as Allaah says (you will find the staunchest enemies of those that have believed are the Jews...) Sura 5:82. So the ever ongoing Jewish enmity towards the Muslims is permanent through the testimony of the Noble Qur'an and fully embedded in the mind and conscience of every Muslim who believes in the Qur'an. His faith in this sense cannot be shaken by anything in this world. This should explain the wave of mockery and (disapproval) of the frivolous peace efforts that are undertaken and are being held under the pretext of peace with the Jews...which will Never ever be!!"[16]

Note that the verses quoted above by Al-Qaradawi reflect Allah's perspective on the Jews, not man's—that Allah has proclaimed the "enmity" to be coming from the Jews, not the other way around, so that the Jews must be seen and treated as permanent enemies—and Al-Qaradawi uses these verses to back up his own opinion of current negotiations, to the effect that the "frivolous peace efforts...are being held under the pretext of peace with the Jews...which will never be!"

In essence, in his speech to the Arabic media the "enmity" he refers to is strictly Qur'anic—based not on anything the Jews have really done, but

---

[15] http://www.khayma.com/internetclinic/yahodman.htm

[16] Here is the original quote as given in Arabic: اليهود هم أعدى أعداء الأمة! وعداوتهم للإسلام
والمسلمين كانت ولا زالت وستظل ما بقى مسلمون ويهود على هذه الأرض قضية مبرمة قضى فيها من أحاط
عاما بما كان ، وبما هو كائن وبما سيكون .. يقول سبحانه (لتجدن أشد الناس عداوة للذين آمنوا اليهود...)-الآية
82 سورة المائدة فعداوة اليهود المستمرة الدائمة للمسلمين أصبحت بشهادة القرآن الكريم و من البديهات
المستقرة في عقل ووجدان وضمير كل مسلم يؤمن بهذا لكتاب وإيمانه بهذه البديهة لا يستطيع أن يغلغله أو يهزه
أي شئ في العالم ، ومن هنا كانت (السخرية) و(الاستنكار) من كل العبثيات التي جرت وتجري تحت دعاوى
السلام مع اليهود ...والذي لن يكون!!

instead on what the Qur'an says they had done in the 7th century—so that there is no court of appeal, and no mercy in regard to what he calls the "pretext" of the negotiations over the "land".

So here the reason for the enmity has nothing whatsoever to do with the political issues or anything the Jews have "done', but instead primarily has to do with the vile "character" of who the Jews "are" according to the Qur'an, a fact which is compounded, and exponentially so— by their very existence and presence on the "land" which presence is seen by the Muslims as an anathema.

However, when speaking to a Western audience, this enmity is usually justified pragmatically, by stating that it is caused by the 1948 Jewish occupation which was later extended in 1967. The argument goes, that since then Israel has taken actions to cause the continuation of this "aggression", such as the building of the defence barrier, settlements on the West Bank, and the 2006 attack on Lebanon and the recent attack on Gaza. In short, this conflict is presented to the West as purely political rather than being firmly rooted in a divinely ordained eternal mandate, as per Al-Qaradawi's statements in Arabic to a Muslim audience condemning the Jews, and to the Western audience denying that "Jewishness" has anything whatsoever to do with it. Again we have the alternating between the religious/Islamic agenda and the pragmatic/political land issues—in order to hide the true intentions and thus we see another effectual smokescreen.

Deploying the "political/pragmatic" rationale, tremendous political pressures from the international community are being brought to bear on Israel, starting from the current USA Secretary of State, Hilary Clinton, and former President Carter, to so many other foreign ministers shuttling to and fro suggesting the imposition of their own political solutions on Israel—insisting that lasting peace would surely come, were a proper Palestinian state (composed of Gaza and the West Bank) to be established, with at least a part of Jerusalem as its capital.

Old questions seen through a new lens

But with the conflicting alternative "religious/Islamic" rationale, as seen through, the lens of "enmity" in the Qur'an towards the Jews, and with the same being openly expressed and affirmed by Muslim religious authorities to Muslim audiences—the question must be posed: "Is the pragmatic approach to solving the land issues viable or even possible?"

So we further ask:

1. If Israel were to accept the above-stated proposal, would that end the hostilities and extinguish the enmity of the Muslims and Arabs towards the Jews and towards Israel?

2. Or would such a move have a reverse impact by forcing an agreement which is diametrically opposed by the Qur'an, and thus by Allah himself, as we just saw—thus deepening the crisis, increasing the enmity and hate, multiplying the terror and rocket attacks several hundred fold?

3. Given that Jerusalem is an admitted bone of contention—one has to ascertain the answer to the question: How is Jerusalem connected to all these?

4. In addition, since we have seen that the Qur'an is written in a way as to shield the true meaning from unbelievers on several other issues, how do we know if there are not further claims to the land coming from within it which would be violated by such an agreement?

All of these questions must be answered in turn, in order to get a grasp of what is really at stake in the current "negotiations" to settle the Arab-Israeli conflict.

Note that each proposed solution above raises a larger question.

Before we begin to consider these questions it is important to point out that from the Islamic point of view, any discussion pertaining to the rights of the Jews is considered to be the most offensive and controversial of topics. In fact, bringing up any issue which debates the "rights" of a Jew is generally perceived in a personal way by the Arabs and Muslims—especially at a street/public level, as the remote possibility that a Jew could have "rights" vis-a-vis a Muslim is an anathema.

Chapter 2
The Myth of Peace: A Two-State Solution

Misleading Perceptions

"*If there were to be an appropriate agreement over the land among the Jews and the Arabs, the crisis would be over*". This oft-repeated "land view" presupposes that the issue is all about some misunderstanding no matter how serious but to a great degree a misunderstanding of "who owns what!" This thinking takes a circular form that ends up favouring the Palestinians. The argument goes that, maybe the Palestinians owned the land more recently, although the Jews owned that very land before them—but then one must consider that the Jews were no longer there at some point, and so the Palestinians may have taken possession of it for a time, so that the returning Jews in the 18th and 19th centuries then had to repurchase it from them.

However, in 1948 when the state of Israel was born, the Jews were already living there in substantial numbers. So those who hold the view that it is all about the land assume that, if

> The **Islamic Smokescreen Response** has two types, the official and the street version, both of which are based on alternating between two sets of mutually contradictory rationales: (a) the political/pragmatic rationale based solely on the "land", and (b) the religious/Islamic rationale based on the Islamic mandates toward the Jews and the land. The only difference is that in the street response both rationales are given intermittently and simultaneously—such that it is difficult to keep track of the line of reasoning.

such is the case then no matter how big a disagreement of who owns what, it might be surmountable, given that both sides want to live in peace. So that in the end, it's only a matter of negotiation—negotiating from who owned what prior to 1948, as that was the crisis point…presupposing that the Arab – Israeli conflict is purely a political crisis which began in the 1940s. But again we ask, is it really?

The Islamic Smokescreen Response brought into focus

Two types of "smokescreen"

There are two types of smokescreen, the first being that of the official spokesmen presenting the Western press or audience with the political/pragmatic "land" rationale, while presenting the Muslim audience with the real reasons, i.e. the "religious/Islamic" rationale. This serves to please the Western public by giving the hope that a political solution is possible, while assuring the rank and file Muslims that indeed the doctrinal line is being held, as we saw earlier in the duplicitous response from Sheikh Al Qaradawi.

This type of official orchestration of the issue between the insiders and the outsiders is not unheard of by politicians, when they can pull it off undetected—as it is meant to keep the focus off the true intent, which in this case, are the simple provable facts of the doctrinal position.

However, the second type of smokescreen may come as a surprise—although it is the same dynamic of alternating between the religious and the pragmatic, but this time in a one-on-one conversation that one may have with any Muslim about the Arab-Israeli conflict.

The standard Islamic "street" response is an example of such a habitual smokescreen. It is always presented in a seemingly logical and orderly fashion—though in reality it is neither of these. Instead, when dissected, it is a mishmash of loosely related or unrelated issues, accusations, and judgements, using all the right terminology—which in turn is connected to unrelated events with great confidence as though it were all related. The end result being an almost incomprehensible total distortion of the issues.

Such responses are narrated authoritatively, using tragic human stories to make themselves appear to be innocent victims of Jewish brutality—

while passionately spinning an account of the incident which ignores the actual factors that led to it, leaves out the historical context in which these events would have occurred, distorts the chronology of events, and generally distorts the truth of the matter in such a way that it is difficult to follow, and almost impossible to un-weave.

In so doing, they seemingly portray the conflict as inhumane and unjust, and as heavy handedness on the part of the Jews towards Muslims and helpless Arab Palestinians. As such, they brilliantly succeed in not only presenting themselves as justified "victims", but also in distancing "wrongdoing" as having any connection with Islam, but rather using the occasion as a golden opportunity to proclaim the goodness of Islam.

In short, the standard presentation of this conflict by a Muslim "on the street" or in a one-on-one discourse with someone in an official capacity is woven in such complexity that it enables them to both obscure the reality of the situation, or the real issues, and to promote Islam favourably—both religiously and politically—while at the same time alternatively using both political and religious dogmas.

This is done to achieve the following objectives for the defence, promotion and propagation of Islam.

1. The defence of Islam

    a. To exonerate Islam and Muslims from all accusations of violence and terrorism.

    b. To establish the "other", in this case the "Jew" as the perpetrator and first "cause" of the retributive acts by Muslims.

    c. Thus to establish themselves as the recipients of unwarranted "enmity" (as per earlier quoted Qur'anic verses attributing the "enmity" as coming "naturally" from the Jews toward Islam instead of the other way around.)

2. Promotion and propagation of Islam

    a. To show that Islam is a "religion of peace,"

    b. To show that Islam "respects" other religions,

    c. To show that Islam is a religion of tolerance,

d. Thus to establish that Islamic Shariah is the best example for humanity, and

e. Thus to grow and empower Muslim communities.

Thus one can see that the defence, promotion and the propagation of Islam is done through the repetitive recitation of a magic mantra "...*Islam is a religion of peace...*", they say, *"though oft misrepresented by those who do not understand, or those who do not follow its peaceful precepts as set by Muhammad."*

While the absolution of Islam and/or Muslims is a paramount objective of such discourse, this goal is always secured by the use of another Mantra of sorts, if more complex—by charging or accusing the Jews/Israeli's/ Americans as the case may be, with violence as initiators and perpetrators who are always at the forefront of all conflicts, and are always engaged in engineering it from behind the scenes.

To achieve the above, two sets of arguments are used intermittently, in unison, and interchangeably: political and religious.

Political arguments and deliberations are based on all kinds of injustices that are imposed on the Muslim Ummah or community worldwide, which is always said to be due to the Israeli occupation of the Palestinian lands, and the support by the Western Imperial and colonial powers, headed by the USA and the Crusader-Zionist occupiers to control of all the precious resources of the region.

Abrogated Qur'anic verses put to use

Simultaneously the religious arguments are woven in throughout, quoting religious texts, declaring Islam to be a peaceful religion which recognizes and respects Judaism and Christianity, while not being respected in return. This technique is totally predictable as emanating directly from Qur'anic verses which would appear to offer forgiveness, peace and tolerance with all the revealed religions, as well as the recognition of these religions while holding them in high esteem. However the verses which would offer all these good things were all abrogated during Muhammad's lifetime and thus are non-effective and no longer valid.

Thus Muslims justify their hostility and deep abiding enmity towards the Jews by employing their arguments of the Jewish original occupation of Palestinian land as reason number one, as well as the resulting continued Jewish aggression on the Palestinians, like that of the recent war in Gaza and all other injustices, as other supporting reasons–leaving out the reality that the Palestinians and the Arabs do provoke, and continue to keep the issue hot and alive.

The Jews, Israel and America as another cover

As Muslims begin to deliberate on Palestine and its occupation, not only the occupied lands of Palestine but all kinds of failures in all the Arab and Islamic states get to be laid at the door of Israel and its Western Crusader Zionist backers as a Zionist conspiracy. They cite obvious non sequitur failures, such as a lack of democracy in almost all Islamic countries, being ruled by dictators, unjust Islamic governments, and every other kind of injustice including the rise in costs of living, lack of good education, and poor infrastructures in some of the Muslim countries, in other words, a long list of all that the Islamic world suffers from, while blaming Israel and the Jews for them all. This includes, believe it or not, blaming them for the 9/11 attacks. Hence all these arguments taken together justify in their mind the Islamic terror against Israel, or America as her backer.

This raises an important question about the history of the Jews in Arabia under Islam. If all the furore is only about the so called occupation of 1948, and related injustices by Israel and its supporters—does that mean that prior to 1948 the Muslims loved the Jews? In fact the larger question is: Was there ever a time when they loved the Jews?

If so, then why were there ongoing and sporadic genocides/pogroms of the Jews by the Muslims since the 7th century? Not just during the formative years of Islam in Medina and the Arabian Peninsula, but for instance the more recent examples in the 18th, 19th and 20th centuries in Persia (Iran), Turkey, the Balkans, Morocco, Tunisia, Syria, Iraq, Egypt, and Palestine itself.[17] These are "open secrets" for those wishing to delve into the

---

[17] For detailed documentation on the pogroms, massacres and abuse of Jews in these see Bat Ye'or, "Islam and Dhimmitude—Where Civilizations Collide," published in 2002.

historicity of the conflict rather than depending upon sanitized versions which minimize, and even obscure, the reality of such occurrences.

In fact, the historical behavioural pattern of Muslims to divert from the root religious cause of enmity to a pragmatic political/emotional cause is well developed and clearly shows that all the Islamic justifications are false excuses raised up against the facts of the situation which can be easily refuted and rejected once examined through the lens of the Qur'an, the Sunnah and the Islamic history, past and present.

Chapter 3
Roots of the Enmity: Grounds for Litigation

The Qur'an puts the focus on the Jews (and Christians)

Whosoever considers, or studies the primary sources of Islam, the Qur'an, the Hadith, the Sira (biography of Muhammad) and the Islamic history that has been penned by the Muslims themselves[18], would be stunned to face such a flood of enmity towards the Jews and the Christians starting from the first Sura of the Qur'an *"those on whom your wrath dwells* (meaning the Jews), *and those that who have gone astray"* (referring to the Christians) till the end of the Qur'anic revelations and the various Hadith of all kinds and forms. In other words, the Islamic sources themselves command its adherents to hate the Jews and the Christians.

There are approximately 700[19] verses in the Qur'an that refer and relate to the Jews and Christians, explicitly, but were we to consider this

---

[18] Arab theologians on Jews and Israel by D. L. Green/ pages 19 – 48 papers by various Islamic scholars. For example, on page 22 and as part of the paper entitled, "The Jews Are the Enemies of Human Life as Is Evident from Their Holy Book," the writer, Dr. Kamal Ahmad Own, Vice Principal of Tanta Institute makes the observation, "…The Jews Will be the Jews: The Jews wicked nature never changes…As a result God punished them…" In another example starting on page 48, His Eminence Sheikh Nadim Al-Jisr, gave a paper under the title, "Good Tidings about the Decisive Battle between Muslims and Israel, in the Light of the Holy Quran, the Prophetic Traditions, and the Foundational Laws of Nature and History," whereby he stipulated that since the Islamic traditions had predicted a final Battle between Islam and the Jews, then a necessary condition for that was the creation of the Jewish state of Israel, since without such a state, whereby the Jews would have been scattered everywhere, would be meaningless. Hence, the creation of Israel is good news and a necessary prerequisite for this final battle in which the Muslims, will of course be victorious and able to annihilate the Jews.

[19] http://www.iidalraid.de/EnOfQuran/Subject/00001/00002/00017/00040/00096.htm

exegetically it would be almost two third of the Qur'an that is well over 4,000 verses referring to the Jews and Christians and by deduction declaring them to be in enmity with the Muslims.

Let's list a few of these Qur'anic verses, and expound where necessary.

Earlier we quoted Al-Qaradawi whereby the prescribed enmity of the Muslims by the Qur'an is clearly stated in Sura 5:82," *Certainly you will find the most violent of people in enmity for those who believe (to be) the Jews and those who are polytheists, Jews and the polytheists are the worst and most venomous enemies of the Muslims."* Al-Qaradawi's opinion carries a great weight in the Muslim

Qur'anic Profile of a Jew and Judaism: Grounds for Litigation

According to pending laws criminalizing religious "stereotyping" or "defamations of religion"—and this is both—had there been international courts, the Jews of the 7th Century and thereafter would have had ample grounds for bringing suit based on the Qur'anic charges and conclusions about the character of the Jew as an individual, and as a race—as being "the worst of Allah's creation". (See body of text)

Ironically, writings in the Qur'an, the Sunnah, and the Sira (biography of Muhammad) would have already fallen foul of these new laws which are being drafted and presented by Islamic countries, and include the Cairo Declaration of Human Rights of 1990 which is challenging the 1948 Universal Declaration of Human Rights—and a newer measure sponsored by Egypt and the United States at the U.N. (See footnotes No.'s 20, 21 and 22).

World as he is the chairman of the Fatwa Council both in Europe and the Middle East. He is the spiritual guide and spiritual father of the Muslim Brotherhood and most of the radical Islamic organizations. Significantly he is also highly respected and revered by the so-called "moderates" who would normally disagree with the radicals.

To the Muslims this verse firmly establishes a revealed truth which they need to heed as the pattern of conduct which can neither be changed nor altered and that is, that the Jews and the polytheists are the most venomous of the enemies of the Muslims.

The application, the effectiveness and the validity of this verse was never limited to the Jews of Arabia at the time of Muhammad but was always meant to be eternal. As is clear from the formation of its syntax which states, that *'you will find'* being future tense, empathic, confirming that this hate and enmity of the Jews and the polytheists towards Muslims is firmly established in the being and the heart of every Jew according to Islamic revelation and belief. This very view is held and expressed by all Muslim scholars and Qur'anic expositors.

Jews and Christians are polytheists

Of course according to the Qur'an, both Jews and Christians are defined as polytheists by nature, as per Sura 9:30-31, " *And the Jews say: Uzair is the son of Allah; and the Christians say: The Messiah is the son of Allah; these are the words of their mouths; they imitate the saying of those who disbelieved before; may Allah destroy them; how they are turned away! They have taken their doctors of law and their monks for lords besides Allah, and (also) the Messiah son of Mary and they were enjoined that they should serve one Allah only, there is no god but He; far from His glory be what they set up (with Him).* "

So according to the Qur'anic revelations Jews and Christians are first, the enemies of Allah, because they are polytheists and secondly, of the Muslims because they have resisted Allah and his Messenger. Added to that, Allah has also revealed their heart, and their natural hatred toward the Muslims. But as it has been pointed out above by Al Qaradawi the Jews however, are the most venomous—as they are enemy number one to all the Muslims. Therefore Allah's directive to the Muslims as follows:

For according to Sura 5:82, "*Certainly you will find the most violent of people in enmity for those who believe (to be) the Jews.*"

Sura 60:1, "*O you who believe! Take not My enemies and your enemies (i.e. disbelievers and polytheists*, in other words Jews and Christians) *as friends, showing affection towards them, while they have disbelieved in what has come to you of the truth.*"

Sura 5:51,"*O ye who believe! Take not the Jews and the Christians for friends. They are friends one to another. He among you who taketh them for friends is (one) of them. Lo! Allah guideth not wrongdoing folk.*"

Allegiance and Rejection: The Islamic doctrine of eternal enmity

Hence these Qur'anic directives point to the revelation of creating of a separate Islamic society, a society whose allegiance is to be given only to Allah and Muhammad. This requires that the Muslim community itself, i.e. the Muslim "Ummah", must remain in a prescribed state of open "enmity" and hostility towards Jews first, then Christians, and finally all non-Muslims, save for short-term pragmatic reasons having to do with the advancement and protection of Islam itself (such as national "allegiance" required by a host society). The authority for this withholding of "allegiance" in response to any political system, or any personal relationship, is set in stone as per the doctrine of Al-Walaa' wa Al-Baraa'.

Al-Walaa' wa Al-Baraa' most simply translated would mean "Allegiance and Rejection"—or the expression of love, or "allegiance" for the sake of Allah and the expression of hate, or "enmity" also for the sake of Allah, i.e. meaning, to both offer and withhold—for the sake of Allah. This is a necessary over-simplification to communicate the essence of the concept, as it is important to get a basic understanding of it first, and then hopefully to gain a firmer grip on this complex doctrinal terminology, as it is the Qur'anic basis for the initial self-segregation of the Muslim "Ummah" within host societies, and at some point in time, the later refusal to obey man-made laws as embodied in the various constitutions outside of Islam.

Think of "allegiance" as giving "commitment, love, and support" for a friend, colleague, or political entity such as a country. Think of "rejection" as not only "refusing" to give such "commitment, love, and support", but in the act of rejecting it, to make the recipient feel not only rejection, but deep and abiding "enmity" or hatred.

Muslim scholars agree that the religious commitment of any Muslim, to Islam can never be regarded as complete, unless he or she takes the necessary steps to visibly show and express "disapproval", or "enmity" towards the unbelievers and polytheists (Including Judaism and Christianity) even if they be close relatives, as stated in the following:

Sura 60:1, *"O you who believe! Take not My enemies and your enemies (i.e. disbelievers and polytheists, etc.) as friends, showing affec-*

tion towards them, while they have disbelieved in what has come to you of the truth (i.e. Islâmic Monotheism, this Qur'ân, and Muhammad),"

Sura 60:4, "*Indeed there has been an excellent example for you in Ibrâhim and those with him, when they said to their people: "Verily, we are free from you and whatever you worship besides Allâh, we have rejected you, and there has started between us and you, hostility and hatred for ever…*"

Sura 58:22, "*You (O Muhammad SAW) will not find any people who believe in Allâh and the Last Day, making friendship with those who oppose and resist Allâh and His Messenger (Muhammad SAW), even though they were their fathers, or their sons, or their brothers, or their kindred (people). For such He has written Faith in their hearts, and strengthened them with Rûh (proofs, light and true guidance) from Himself. And We will admit them to Gardens (Paradise) under which rivers flow, to dwell therein (forever). Allâh is pleased with them, and they with Him. They are the Party of Allâh (Hizbullah). Verily, it is the Party of Allâh (Hizbullah) that will be the successful.*"

Sura 3:28," *Let not the believers take for friends or helpers Unbelievers rather than believers: if any do that, in nothing will there be help from Allah: except by way of precaution, that ye may Guard yourselves from them. But Allah cautions you (To remember) Himself; for the final goal is to Allah*".

Sura 9:23, "*O you who believe! Take not for Auliya' (supporters and helpers) your fathers and your brothers if they prefer disbelief to Belief. And whoever of you does so, then he is one of the wrong-doers.*"

Sura 3:118, "*O you who believe! Take not as (your) advisors, consultants, protectors, helpers, friends, those outside your religion (pagans, Jews, Christians, and hypocrites) since they will not fail to do their best to corrupt you. They desire to harm you severely. Hatred has already appeared from their mouths, but what their breasts conceal is far worse. Indeed We have made plain to you the Ayat if you understand.*"

Hence "love" and/or "allegiance" is only to be given within the framework of the Islamic community, but "rejection", "hate" and "enmity" are mandatory in responding to those outside the framework of the Islamic community—and thus both responses are fundamental ingredients or components of the Qur'anic teaching, of which Al-Walaa' wa Al-Baraa' is the core doctrine[20].

Long-range implications: The enmity is eternal

To understand the long range and lasting implications of the above verses and the Doctrine of Allegiance and Rejection one must ask a further question: What is the lifespan of this prescribed enmity? One needs to pose an appropriate question to Muslims worldwide and to their eminent scholars: Who are the Jews and the Christians that the Muslims have been forbidden by the Qur'anic revelations to take as friends? Were they the Jews and the Christians of the time of Muhammad only? Or are they the Jews and the Christians of all times past, present and future throughout time?

If these verses were limited in time and meant only for the Jews and the Christians at the time of Muhammad, then does that mean that these verses have expired and are thus non-effective and can now be treated as historical archives, past their sale date, and are not to be implemented?

However if these verses remain in force and are currently applicable to the Jews and the Christians of this age, doesn't this constitute a direct and explicit "incitement" of the hatred of the "other" i.e., "non-Muslims?" Ironically, this "incitement", recognized for what it is—might qualify as grounds for prosecution under the proposed and current hate crime legislation in the West.

> If these Quranic verses quoted herein remain in force and are currently applicable to the Jews and the Christians of this age, doesn't this constitute a direct and explicit "incitement" of the hatred of the "other" i.e., "non-Muslims?"

If these verses are still in force, wouldn't this Qur'anic stereotyping fall foul of the Cairo Declaration of Human Rights of 1990[21] which is chal-

---

[20] http://www.scribd.com/doc/7706435/AL-Wala-Wal-Bara-2-and-3-by-Shaykh-Muhammad-Saeed-Al-Qahtani

[21] http://www.religlaw.org/interdocs/docs/cairohrislam1990.htm

lenging the 1948 Universal Declaration of Human Rights[22]—and a newer measure sponsored by Egypt and the United States[23] at the U.N.? And if so, don't these verses function as a fundamental guideline and a continuous mandate, thus being an indispensible factor in the destruction of a Muslim's relationship with a non-Muslim? What are the implications?

Hence, a question to all those who claim that the hatred of the Jews by the Arabs and the Muslims is due solely to the Jewish occupation. If the occupation were ended would that change the Qur'anic verse of Sura 5:51, "*O ye who believe! Take not the Jews and the Christians for friends. They are friends one to another. He among you who taketh them for friends is (one) of them. Lo! Allah guideth not wrongdoing folk.*"

To something like: "*O ye who believe! Take the Jews and the Christians for friends. He among you who does not take them for friends is amongst the wrong doers. Lo! Allah guideth not wrongdoing folk.*"

In other words, would we then see a fatwa from the most learned Islamic scholars declaring the invalidity and inapplicability of the above-mentioned verse?

Portrayal of the Jews in the Qur'an

As stated before, the Qur'an seems to focus on the Jews like no other, and so it – the Qur'an—has devoted a very large portion and percentage of the entire text to the Jews, well over half and close to 60%. Noting that the Qur'an has a total of 114 chapters called "Sura's" of varying lengths, and a total of 6,666 verses[24], called "Aya's," we calculate that the total number of chapters or Suras in which direct and explicit references are made towards

---

[22] http://www.aspire-irl.org/UN_Universal_Declaration_of_Human_Rights.pdf

[23] http://daccessddsny.un.org/doc/RESOLUTION/GEN/G09/166/89/PDF/G0916689.pdf? OpenElement: Third Committee Approves Resolution Aimed at 'Combating Defamation of Religions', One of 16 Draft Texts Recommended to General Assembly Refugee High Commissioner, Globalization, Disabilities Convention, Palestinian Self-Determination, Protecting Migrants Among Other Issues Addressed

[24] The total number of verses are 6666, as per Chapter 2 page 21 of "Shariah: the Islamic Law" by Abur Rahman I., Doi Published by Taha publishers Ltd London UK ISBN 0-907461-04-2. In general, Muslim scholars differ in the methods of counting the verses of the Qur'an, hence the numbers vary from 6236 to 6349 to 6448 to what Professor Doi has stated 6666.

the Jews include over 50 out of the 114 Suras in total, which constitutes almost 44% of the chapters of the Qur'an. The following is a list of those 50 plus Qur'anic chapters, or Suras, where there are direct references to the Jews and Christians: Sura's 1, 2, 3, 4, 5, 6, 7, 8, 9, 10, 11,12, 14, 16, 17, 18,19, 20,21, 22, 23, 24, 25, 26,27, 28, 29, 30, 31, 33, 34,39,40, 42, 43, 44, 45, 46, 56,57, 58, 59, 60, 61, 62, 63, 64, 73, 98, 109, 113, and 114.

But that is not the whole extent because of the widely varying lengths of the Sura's. As we shall see in some cases, almost entire Sura's are devoted to the subject.

In total, some 4,000, or roughly 60% of the 6,666 Aya's contain either direct or indirect reference to the issue of the Jews. Of the direct Aya's, only 3% (around 200 Aya's) of this total are somewhat neutral references many of which are later abrogated, leaving 7.5% (or around 500 Aya's) as attributing some of the ugliest descriptions possible, singling out the Jews as the worst segment of humanity.

The remaining indirect references are equally condemnatory but are veiled in such a way that one must consult the "Tafsir" or expert commentary to discover the depth of the enmity being expressed.

It must be noted however that there are other competing estimates of the total number of Aya's or verses in the Qur'an—ranging from 6236 to 6349 to 6448, to 6666 as used above. Note that if one were to use one of the lower estimates — as the basis for the above calculations, that would provide an even higher percentage of verses expressing enmity toward the Jews. At the lower end the percentage would increase by 4 points from 60% to 64%.

Let's remind ourselves once again that, were we to consider the above exegetically, taking onboard the implicit references as well as the explicit, it would constitute almost two thirds of the entire Qur'an—that is well over 4000 (four thousand) verses, or 60-64%, which directly refer to the Jews (and Christians) in one way or another, and by a combination of induction and deduction, declare them to be in divinely mandated eternal enmity with the Muslims.[25]

---

[25] For more details see Chapter 4, "Challenges from Islam" by Sam Solomon, in the book, *Beyond Opinion*, by Ravi Zacharias, Author and General Editor, Thomas Nelson, Publisher, Nashville, TN, (2007).

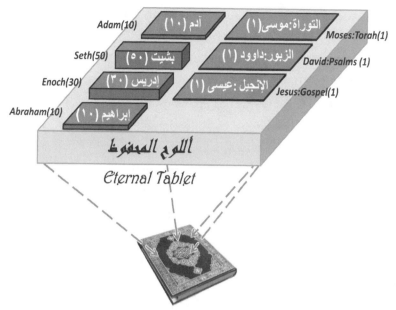

Eternal Tablet (Source of the Qur'an)

Figure 1: Islam teaches that the Qur'an is eternal and is preserved in the "eternal tablet"(Sura 85:21-22) —and is said to have "come down" in stages, the last three books being the Torah, the Psalms, and the Gospel, but reached its final form as we know it today during Muhammad's ministry. Thus in Islam the Qur'an has replaced all previous books including the 100 unknown and the three known "revealed books" as shown in the diagram.[26]

Just by way of example, here we illustrate some key verses (Aya's) from among the 500 direct and explicit negative references to Jews, taken from only eight Sura's (chapters), 1, 2, 3, 4, 5, 7, 8, and 9. These verses are summarized to the key points. (But the full text of each verse can be seen in the Appendix A).

---

[26] "The Jews in the Qur'an" by Professor Addul Sattar El Sayed the Mufti of Turso Syria; Arab Theologians on Jews and Israel 1968 conference, summation by Green. In fact the author of this article quotes many of the same references given herein under such headings as: "Telling lies about God; Their fondness to listening to falsehood (lies); Mutiny (disobedience) against Allah; Hard-heartedness;…;Hypocrisy…; Desire for corrupting people…; Exploitation and opportunism…; Trickery for transgression; Cowardice; Indecency in talking; Miserliness…; The most excessive selfishness…; Garbling of the holy books".

A. Allah's key charges and judgments against the Jews (and Christians) (selected):

- Sura 9:30, Jews associated a son (Uzayr) to Allah..." (Shirk, i.e. polytheism)
- Sura 7:138, "Jews were calf worshippers..." (Idol worshippers)
- Sura 9:31,"Jews took their leaders as gods instead of Allah..." (Shirk, i.e. polytheism)
- Sura 5:64, Sura 3:181, "Jews reproached Allah..." (In rebellion against Allah)
- Sura 2:87, Sura 5:70, "...the Jews are prophet killers..." (In rebellion)
- Sura 2:100, Sura 5:13, "Jews are covenant breakers, full of treason, vengeful..." (In rebellion)
- Sura 5:79," the Jews made lawful all that was forbidden..." (Rebellion, Lawless People)
- Sura 4:51-52, "Jews practising sorcery and witchcraft..." (Evildoers)
- Sura 5:64, "Jews are igniters of fires of war..." (Rebellion, Lawless People)
- Sura 5:62, 17:4, "Jews are corrupters on earth,..." (Rebellion, Lawless People)
- Sura 2:75f, Sura 4:46, "The Jews corrupted the scriptures..." (Corruptors of scriptures)
- Sura 2:42, "Jews conceal truth with falsehood..." (Corruptors of scriptures)
- Sura 9:32, "Jews tried to extinguish Allah's light..." (Corruptors of scriptures)
- Sura 3:183-184, "Jews are liars..." (Immoral character)
- Sura 2:93-96, "Jews are cowards, protective of their lives, they don't fight except from behind fortresses..." (Immoral character)
- Sura 4:161, "Jews are devourers and chargers of usury..." (Immoral character)

- Sura 5:62, "Jews are lovers of transgression and sin..." (Immoral character)
- Sura 2:142, "Jews are vulgar and fools..." (Immoral character)
- Sura 5:64, "Jews are haters of one another and full of enmity to their own..." (Immoral character)
- Sura 2:145, Sura 7:132, "Jews are hard hearted..." (Irredeemable hearts)
- Sura 2:74, 88, "...Jews' hearts are harder then stones..." (Irredeemable hearts)

B. Allah's judgments, curses and penalties against the Jews (selected):
- Sura 1:7, "Jews are people on whom is the wrath of Allah," (Cursed by Allah)
- Sura 4:51-52, "...whosoever is cursed by Allah will find himself no helper..." (Rejection of Muslims and therefore, cursed by Allah)
- Sura 7:152, Jews deserve "...wrath from their Lord and humiliation will come upon them..." (Cursed by Allah)
- Sura 58:14, The Jews are "...a people upon whom is the wrath of Allâh..." (Cursed by Allah)
- Sura 2:65, 5:60, 7:166, "Jews are those who were cursed and transformed into apes and swine..." (Cursed and judged by Allah)
- Sura 2:61, Sura 3:112, "...they drew on themselves the Wrath of Allâh...because they used to disbelieve the proofs..." (Cursed and judged by Allah)
- Sura 8:55- 56, 98:6, " Jews are the worst of Allah's creation..." (Allah final judgment)

As stated at the beginning of this section, these are but a fraction of the most abusive, discriminatory, and degrading descriptions attributed to the Jews by Allah himself from among the 4,000 verses which in some way refer to the them individually, or collectively as a race but these examples do not include the milder expressions of condemnations or those verses that contain innuendos of condemnations.

The preceding is only a taste of what has been revealed in the Qur'an alone about the character of the Jews, but let's now consider some key aspects of what is contained in the Sunnah/Hadith (the example of Muhammad by word, deed or consent), regarding the Jews, and the policies which were initially set to regulate the relationship of Muslims with the Jews and the Christians.

Portrayal of the Jews According to the Sunnah and Hadith

First, let us explain what is meant by the Sunnah and the Hadith. It is critical to get a handle on this complex subject in order to comprehend how a Muslim's life is regulated and controlled by the combination of the Qur'an and the Sunnah/Hadith—as these are the primary sources of Islamic authority.

Figure 2: Picture of "Sahih Al-Bukhari" which is one of the authoritative Hadith manuscripts. Note that the Hadith books are much more voluminous than the Qur'an. The primary sources of the Shariah are the Qur'an and the Sunnah.

The Sunnah is called the "Sunnat An-Nabi"-meaning the "Example of the Prophet". The word Sunnah means in English "to shape, to mould, a tract, a path", so that the express purpose of the Sunnah is for one to be moulded, shaped, or formed according to a pattern, by following the example of the Prophet, so that one is eventually transformed.

In essence, Muhammad is the "Exemplar", or "example" or "model" for all mankind. The Hadith is defined as meaning "to talk, speech, narration, and storytelling" and is the communicated expression of the Sunnah. Thus the Hadith would be the expression of what Muhammad did, said, and consented to. The Hadith is thus a collection of several thousand stories and examples of how Muhammad handled situations from the simplest aspect of how to dress, wash, eat, pray, to the deeper issues of Jihad and of the necessity of "enmity" toward the Jews first, and the "other". This body of knowledge about Muhammad's thought and actions were communicated by his companions to their successors, and thereafter by the successors of the successors, and so on. In other words, the Hadith became the vehicle communicating the Sunnah.

For non-Muslims it is difficult to get one's head around this concept, but it could be thought of in a simplistic way as the Hadith being the "means" or mechanism for the desired transformation of the individual, and the Sunnah being the stated "goal"—purpose—to be conformed to the character of Muhammad. In short, one could think of the Hadith as the means, and the Sunnah as the end.

Let's take these three examples of the Sunnah/Hadith in order:

1. <u>By word</u>: The record is clear that—with few exceptions—he treated the Jews harshly by calling them vile and humiliating names. As an example, in negotiating the terms of the first cases wherein two Jewish tribes in Yathrib/Medina were expelled en masse (Banu Kaynuka, and Banu Nadir), and the subsequent terms of surrender for the Jewish tribes of Khaybar, he engaged in harsh verbal treatment.

2. <u>By deed</u>: One example would be the merciless execution of individuals who criticized him from within the third Yathrib/Medina tribe (Banu Qurayza), and the subsequent corporate execution of the male tribesmen. These first few instances—three tribes in Yathrib/Medina, and the tribes of the city of Khaybar—set his policy of either conversion, exile, death, or political subjugation in the most humiliating of terms. In particular, the methods of execution by "be-heading" which were first applied in some of these cases

became the standard, a standard which was emulated in line with the Sunnah in the modern case of Daniel Pearl, the New York Times correspondent who was beheaded in Pakistan. And,

3. <u>By consent</u>: (Incorporating or endorsing traditions, practices, of pre-Islamic Arabia—or from other peoples, like the Jews, or even suggestions from his followers). As an example, Muhammad endorsed the judgment of one of his leaders, Sa'd ibn Mu'adh, chief of the Banu Aus tribe at the Battle of the Ditch in Yathrib/Medina when he, Muhammad upheld Mu'adh's verdict to behead 800 Jewish males of Banu Qurayza, carried out under humiliating circumstances too graphic to describe herein[27].

In the foregoing we have introduced you to three initial examples of the sorts of Hadiths which relate to the Jews, according to the three designations of <u>word</u>, <u>deed</u>, and <u>by consent</u> in order to introduce you to the rationale. Below you will find further examples which reflect some of the most vile references to the Jews in the Sunnah/Hadith. Note that combinations of two or more, such as "<u>deed</u> and <u>word</u>" or "<u>deed, word,</u> and <u>by consent</u>" indicate the strength and importance of the Sunnah in regulating Muslims' behaviour.

Greetings (negative, displaying enmity) to Jews and Christians

"Muhammad the messenger of Allah said, 'Do not greet Jews or Christians with peace if you meet one of them in your way then push them over to a ditch or a narrow path'" Hadith Number 4030 Reported by Al Muslim. [28] (<u>deed</u> and <u>word</u>)

---

[27] http://www.answering-islam.org/Muhammad/Jews/BQurayza/banu2.html

[28] http://hadith.al-islam.com/Display/Display.asp?Doc=1&Rec=5180:

حدثنا قتيبة بن سعيد حدثنا عبد العزيز يعني الدراوردي عن سهيل عن أبيه عن أبي هريرة
أن رسول الله صلى الله عليه وسلم قال لا تبدءوا اليهود ولا النصارى بالسلام فإذا لقيتم أحدهم في طريق فاضطروه إلى أضيقه
و حدثنا محمد بن المثنى حدثنا محمد بن جعفر حدثنا شعبة ح و حدثنا أبو بكر بن أبي شيبة وأبو كريب قالا حدثنا وكيع عن سفيان ح و حدثني زهير بن حرب حدثنا جرير كلهم عن سهيل بهذا الإسناد وفي حديث وكيع إذا لقيتم اليهود وفي حديث ابن جعفر عن شعبة قال في أهل الكتاب وفي حديث جرير إذا لقيتموهم ولم يسم أحدا من المشركين

Muhammad commanded his followers to curse the Jews and the Christians

Muslims are also commanded to curse Jews and Christians following the practice of Muhammad as reported by Bukhari Hadith number 3195[29] *"May the curse of Allah be on the Jews and the Christians who took the graves of their prophets to be as places of worship."* (deed and word)

Allah substituting a Jew or a Christian in hell for a Muslim

"From the Prophet who said when a Muslim man dies Allah sends in his place a Jew or Christian as a substitution," reported by Sahih al Muslim, repentance chapter, Hadith number 4970[30], chapter on the acceptance of the repentance of a Muslim murderer no matter how many he would have murdered. (word)

Allah lays sins of Muslim on Jews and Christians

"As for the prophet who said that on the day of resurrection there will be Muslims with sins like mountains on them, so Allah will forgive them by placing these sins on the Jews and the Christians," reported by Sahih Al Muslim Hadith number 4971[31], repentance chapter. (word)

Muhammad gives "consent" for killing one of his critics

"A Jewess used to abuse [i.e. write satirical verses about] the Prophet (PBUH) and disparage him. A man strangled her till she died. The Apostle of Allah (PBUH) declared that no recompense was payable for her blood." (Bk. 38, No. 4349: Narrated by Ali Ibn Abi Talib). (consent)

---

[29] http://hadith.al-islam.com/Display/Display.asp?Doc=0&Rec=5317:

حدثني بشر بن محمد أخبرنا عبد الله أخبرني معمر ويونس عن الزهري قال أخبرني عبيد الله بن عبد الله أن عائشة وابن عباس رضي الله عنهم قالا

لما نزل برسول الله صلى الله عليه وسلم طفق يطرح خميصة على وجهه فإذا اغتم كشفها عن وجهه فقال وهو كذلك لعنة الله على اليهود والنصارى اتخذوا قبور أنبيائهم مساجد يحذر ما صنعوا

[30] http://hadith.al-islam.com/Display/Dislpay.asp?Doc=1&Rec=63996

[31] http://hadith-islam.com/Display/Display.asp?Doc=1&Rec=6397

Muhammad asserts that Jews and Christians were not faithful and deserve no reward from Allah even for their custodianship

The Prophet said, *"The example of Muslims, Jews and Christians is like the example of a man who employed laborers to work for him from morning till night. They worked till mid-day, and they said, 'We are not in need of your reward.' So the man employed another batch, and said to them, 'Complete the rest of the day and yours will be the wages I had fixed (for the first batch).' They worked up till the time of the 'Asr prayer and said, 'Whatever we have done is for you.' He employed another batch. They worked for the rest of the day till sunset, and they received the wages of the two former batches."* (Vol. 1, bk. 10, No. 53: Narrated by Abu Musa) (word). [This Hadith is very reminiscent of a New Testament Parable of the vineyard laborers, except all laborers get wages in Jesus's parable (Matthew 20:1-16)[32]].

Case where Muhammad copies the Jews in fasting while maintaining his supremacy

"The Prophet came to Medina and saw the Jews fasting on the day of Ashura. He asked them about that. They replied, 'This is a good day, a day

---

[32] This New Testament parable is known as the "Labourers in the Vineyard" and goes as follows, "1 For the kingdom of heaven is like a landowner who went out early in the morning to hire labourers for his vineyard. 2 When he had agreed with the labourers for a denarius for the day, he sent them into his vineyard. 3 And he went out about the third hour and saw others standing idle in the market place; 4 and to those he said, 'You also go into the vineyard, and whatever is right I will give you.' And so they went. 5 Again he went out about the sixth and the ninth hour, and did the same thing. 6 And about the eleventh hour he went out and found others standing around; and he said to them, 'Why have you been standing here idle all day long?' 7 They said to him, because no one hired us.' He said to them, 'You go into the vineyard too.' 8 When evening came, the owner of the vineyard said to his foreman, 'Call the labourers and pay them their wages, beginning with the last group to the first.' 9 When those hired about the eleventh hour came, each one received a denarius. 10 When those hired first came, they thought that they would receive more; but each of them also received a denarius. 11 When they received it, they grumbled at the landowner, 12 saying, 'These last men have worked only one hour, and you have made them equal to us who have borne the burden and the scorching heat of the day.' 13 But he answered and said to one of them, 'Friend, I am doing you no wrong; did you not agree with me for a denarius? 14 'Take what is yours and go, but I wish to give to this last man the same as to you. 15 'Is it not lawful for me to do what I wish with what is my own? Or is your eye envious because I am generous?' 16 So the last shall be first, and the first last." [Matthew 20:1-16, NASB]

on which Allah rescued Bani Israel from their enemy. So, Moses fasted that day.' The Prophet said, 'We have more claim over Moses than you.' So, the Prophet fasted on that day and ordered (the Muslims) to fast (on that day)." Vol. 3, bk. 31, No. 222: Narrated by Ibn Abbas) (word and deed)

Some other critical cases wherein Muhammad copies the Jews

Interestingly enough Jibril, or Gabriel the angel of communication was first mentioned in Medina after Muhammad's close encounter with the Jews.[33] Not only that but virtually almost all of the Islamic religious practices were instituted in Medina, amongst which was ritual prayer, ablution and many others imitating the Jews. These are no small matters! It may come as a surprise that such foundational practices and doctrines as these listed above came some 13 years—well over halfway—into Muhammad's entire mission, and then only during the brief period of time in Medina when he had close and relatively benign relationships with the Jews.

The foregoing was but a few examples from the Qur'an and the vocalized Sunnah, which clearly demonstrate that the issue of the land isn't the fundamental and the sole reason for the hatred and enmity of the Muslims toward the Jews—but instead the "enmity" toward the Jews predated and precipitated the land issues, and this from the perspective of Muhammad, not the Jews. In fact, we will demonstrate that the "expression of enmity" toward the Jews is so foundational, that it is one of the most important doctrines to establish in a Muslim's life in order to consolidate one's Islamic identity. Even when attributing anything positive to the Jews, Muhammad always maintained the upper hand as illustrated in the last two examples above.

Keep in mind that the problem is not limited to the original condemnatory descriptions portrayed in the above references in the Qur'an and Hadith, but instead, the Islamic belief and doctrine is constantly being instilled as a part of their daily religious practice and belief—to reinforce that these character traits and conditions of the heart are uniformly found

---

[33] Sura 2:97-98. This Sura is one of the early Medina Suras and hence the conclusion in the text regarding the first mention of Gabriel.

in every Jew without exception, and will continue to be so in every Jew forever until the day of resurrection.

The mechanisms for keeping the Qur'anic and Sunnah/Hadith "mandates" as a part of the group think of the Muslim Ummah is accomplished mainly through contemporary leadership in pointing back to what the primary sources say, and reinforcing the unavoidable obligation to act on it. Thus the following opinions of current Islamic scholars are critical in understanding how the roots of the "enmity" in the source documents are kept front row centre in the minds of the Muslim on the street.

Portrayal of the Jews in the Sira (biography of Muhammad)

As it is known that no true biography of Muhammad exists in the sense that the earliest one came some 200 years after his death. Added to that the plight of all the fabricated Hadith and the torching of all the variant readings of the Qur'an and its manuscripts by Uthman bin Affaan, as well as the liquidating of all vocal and visible opposition.

This being the case we think it would be inappropriate to refer to the existing documents giving them credence as though these were accurate and reliable. As almost all the significant and relevant materials have been included at some point in this book, and to avoid repeating it over it is only appropriate to suffice ourselves with this passing reference.

Portrayal of the Jews by Contemporary Muslim Scholars[34]

Sheikh Mudathir Ahmed Ismael[35] states in his research titled "*The Doctrine of the Jews in Treaties and Covenants*" says that "*...the Qur'an has not spoken of any as much as it has spoken of Jews, the children of*

---

[34] Arab Theologians on Jews and Israel edited by D.L. Green. The Fourth conference on the Academy of Islamic Research 1976. This book contains some of the vilest descriptions of the Jews in every single paper. Interestingly it quotes President Anwar Sadat in a speech he gave on 25th April, 1972, saying, "...They are a nation of liars and traitors, contrivers of plots, a people born for deeds of treachery...they shall return and be as the Qur'an said of them 'condemned to humiliation and misery' ...We shall send then back to their former status."

[35] http://www.meshkat.net/new/contents.php?catid=5&artid=5201

Israel." He goes on to say that one cannot find in the book of Allah any community whose news and diverse details in its variety are detailed, one after the other, as much as this community, namely the Jews. "Allah has exposed their evil desires, (heart condition) and their vicious temperaments (character) and their enmity to the whole universe, their jealousy of those that do good and seek the truth in all places and at all times and in all ages."

Sheikh Ismael goes on to state that, *"...what we need to point out is when proclaiming the Qur'anic witness or testimony about the Jews is that the Noble Qur'an has verified and ascertained that these descriptions of the Jews and their temperaments are valid and unchanging as it was in the past so it is presently. For the Qur'anic verses tie the Jews who were contemporaries of the prophet and their forefathers with a firm tie as though it was affirming their characteristics, conduct, behaviours and their stand or approaches was and is the proof of what they are and their naturally created makeup being passed on and inherited by the children from their fathers and forefathers".*[36]

While this sounds extreme, it is actually being said by several so-called "moderate" and highly respectable authorities.

A well-known Algerian Muslim scholar, Dr. Sheikh Saffer Bin Abdel Rahman Al Hawali states in his research published on the net[37] entitled *"Jews Are Jews"*: *"The Jews are the Jews who worshipped a calf, and those of Kaynuka, Nadir, and Qurayza and the Jews of Khaybar, whose scandals remain uncountable and their ugliness to Jertesel and his gang is incomprehensible. Menachem Begin and his wickedness and the butchers who came after them for they all — the Jews — are butchers."*

Sheikh Al Qaradawi[38] in explaining the characters of the Jews says, *"...they are full of venom of malice, deception, breakers of covenants, and treaties, and all these has been mentioned by the Qur'an about them, clar-*

---

[36] http://www.meshkat.net/new/contents.php?catid=5&artid=5201

[37] http://www.alhawali.com/index.cfm?method=home.SubContent&contentID=58

[38] http://www.qaradawi.net/site/topics/article.asp?cu_no=2&item_no=178&version=1&template_id=108&parent_id=15#

http://www.qaradawi.net/site/topics/article.asp?cu_no=2&item_no=178&version=1&template_id=108&parent_id=15#%D9%8A%D9%87%D9%88%D8%AF

ifying that the Jews of yesterday are the Jews of today, they hold the same characteristics and temperaments."

Qur'anic passages on the Jews seen as further proof of its miraculous nature

Significantly, Muslims view the Qur'anic passages on the Jews as a further proof of the miraculous nature of the Qur'an in revealing the evil nature of the Jewish heart, as only Allah knows man's heart. Oddly enough, instead of being concerned over the severity of the judgments, to them the Qur'an has embodied the reality of an absent event (i.e. it had not surfaced before) namely the reality of the struggle with the Jews, exposing the personalities of the Jews, their evil nature, the corruption of their beings and their most lowly behaviours.

In other words these Qur'anic verses, their directives, and verdict of final judgment on the Jews is continuous and remains valid and effective even today, and until Allah makes his faithful slaves inherit the earth.

Islamically speaking even elements of nature will participate in the implementation of the judgment or killing of the Jews: Muhammad said that *"The hour will not come until Muslims fight and kill the Jews and the Jews will hide behind trees and rocks, and these trees and rocks will cry out saying, O Muslim, slave of Allah this Jew is hiding behind me, come and kill him."* (Reported by Muslim, Hadith no 5203[39]).

Based on the foregoing it would be correct to conclude that Islamic enmity towards the Jews is of an eternal nature and thus it is here to stay forever.

Implementation of Allah's judgements

The implementation of this judgement started with the purging of the Arabian Peninsula from the Jews and the Christians, and is obligatory on all Muslims. As reported by Umar ibn al Khatab (who later became the second Khalifah) who heard it from the apostle of Allah saying, *"I will*

---

[39] http://hadith.al-islam.com/Display/Display.asp?Doc=1&Rec=6699

expel Jews and Christians from the Arabian Peninsula until there is none but Muslims in it," (Sahih Al Muslim, Hadith no 3313)[40], Book of Jihad, Section on the Expulsion of the Jews and the Christians from the Arabian Peninsula. The Hadith manuals are arranged in categories—as these categories (or chapters) range from personal hygiene to personal relationships, to religious obligations. The Book of Jihad, or the Category of Jihad appears under, "Religious Obligations." In one of its subsections the expulsion of the Jews and the Christians from the Arabian Peninsula is ordered. Hence, it is a religious obligation on all Muslims.

Consequently, based on the above, one can see that the current ongoing demand of Bin Laden and Al Zawaheri to expel the non Muslims from the Arabian Peninsula is solidly grounded in Islamic sources. It is similarly clear from the non-negotiable Saudi government position of a total prohibition and ban on the building of churches or synagogues—even though they are clearly needed by the substantial expatriate community. So the difference between the Bin Laden's and Al-Zawaheri's and the Saudi government is only cosmetic but the form in which Saudi's present it seems more tolerable by the governments of the West—though it is nothing but another form of an Islamic humiliation of non-Muslims. In other words, the demands of Bin Laden and the policy on the ground vary only in degree and appearance—the substance however, remains the same.

This raises an important question: How can Muslims be expected to show any respect towards Jews or Christians when their guiding light, the Qur'an and the Sunnah, constantly reinforced by their top religious leadership—addresses them with such insulting terms…accuses them of such serious offenses against Allah and mankind…and goes so far as to pronounce Allah's judgments and curses on them as the "most despicable of Allah's creation"?

Therefore, having accused and pronounced Allah's judgment on the Jews as a whole—what rights would they have in any area of life, much less in regard to the land? Again we see that the enmity predates land

---

[40] http://hadith.al-islam.com/Display/Display.asp?Doc=1&Rec=4259

issues, and is the reason for the conflict over the land, rather than the land being the reason for the "enmity".

The enmity is a non-augmentable obligation

Thus we have established that the enmity of the Muslims towards the Jews is deeply rooted in the religion itself, in the Qur'an and the Sunnah, and as such is a non-augmentable religious decree.

In other words, in Islamic law, "non-augmentable" is the ultimate case of non-negotiable—in that it is an absolute ruling that cannot even be considered to be changeable...it is the unthinkable...it is beyond the possibility of change, exception, or mercy. The only legal system in the world that has this legal designation is the Hudud section of Islamic law as derived from the Qur'an and the Sunnah in which the judge is barred from even considering mercy should he wish to do so. (This is the right of Allah and no man can contradict it as in Sura 24:2, "...*let no mercy or compassion move you in the religion of Allah...*".) The principle of NO MERCY is established and applied here.[41]

The enmity is the driver of the political conflict over "land"

Since the enmity toward the Jews is a religious decree—and thus an immutable or non-augmentable requirement for every Muslim, emanating from deep religious doctrinal roots, (dogma) as based on the revelations claimed to have been given by Allah to Muhammad—the "enmity" can now be seen to be the driver of the political conflict over the "land" between Israel and the Palestinians, rather than the "cause." So that, the mere thought of having the "hated" Jews living on what is claimed to be Muslim land is the ultimate insult to Islam, not just to the Palestinians.

With this in mind, even if the Israelis were at peace with the Palestinians—based on the foregoing—aren't all Muslims commanded by the Qur'anic injunctions and the Hadith, to continue to execute Allah's eternal

---

[41] In Islamic Jurisprudence the non-augmentable enmity toward the Jews come under the principles deduced from various doctrines, in this case, from Al-Walaa' wa Al-Baraa', the Enemies of Muhammad, thus the Enemies of Allah, and other doctrines.

decree of "enmity" toward the Jews?   And if so, how could one negotiate from the premise of a divinely inspired and commanded enmity?

These implications are currently being acted out in real time in the so-called "Arab-Israeli" conflict though it is said to be "only a conflict over land, social justice, and humanitarian concerns".

Though there admittedly have been massive "humanitarian" casualties in the various wars and skirmishes—it is chilling to realize that it is through the obedience of divinely decreed ordinances to kill "the enemy" (the Jews) that a Muslim pleases Allah, comes close to him, and will thus be regarded as pious by his/her peers in this world for such obedience —while anticipating rewards in the hereafter from Allah.

With this enhanced understanding of the background reality, and result-ant increasing conditions of fear and threats made by those pious and faith-ful Muslims who are most obedient to Allah—how can the international community think that imposing a Two-State solution in the hopes of solv-ing the "land" issue alone could ever put an end to this endemic "enmity", or bring any form of lasting peace?

We will make the case in the next chapter that the "enmity" within the source books is not only the source of the conflict over the "land" in the localized conflict between the Israeli's and Palestinians, but also is the basis for the little understood wider conflict between Islam and the Jews as will be discussed in more depth in the following chapter: Jihad Against the Jews.

Portrayal of the Jews by "fiat"

The "Nakbah" triggers the "fiat" of the Islamic theologians

According the Webster's dictionary the word "fiat" basically means "an authoritative or arbitrary order : decree or dicate…"[42]. This definition fits the determinations at the 1968 "Fourth Conference of the Academy of Islamic Research" held at Al-Azhar University in Cairo. Under the title, "Arab Theologians on Jews and Israel" the writer, D. F. Green summa-

---

[42] http://www.merriam-webster.com/dictionary/fiat

rized the proceedings of this conference which was held just one year after the 1967 defeat and considered by them as the ultimate catastrophe, i.e. Nakbah. Quoting from Mr. Green in his introduction, we briefly cite the "recurring themes" consisting of:

1. "Jews are frequently denoted as the '*Enemies of Allah*[43]' or the '*Enemies of humanity*'..."

2. "Jews manifest in themselves as an historical continuity of evil qualities..."

3. "The Jews are a riff-raff and do not constitute a true people or nation..."

4. "The State of Israel is the culmination of the historical and cultural depravity of the Jews..."

> **The Nakbah**
>
> The loss of Palestine and subsequent loss of Jerusalem to non-Muslims, and even worse, to the Jews, is seen as the ultimate anathema to Islam and thus is termed as, "The Nakbah," or "The Catastrophe."This has given the Muslim theologians their long sought after opportunity—to unilaterally declare by "fiat" the new struggle, i.e. confirmation of the Jihad as proclaimed in the Qur'an and the Sunnah/ Hadith.

5. "The superiority of Islam over all other religions is brandished as a guarantee that the Arabs will ultimately triumph..."

6. "Many participants reiterate that it is outrageous for the Jews, traditionally kept by Arab Islam in a humiliated, inferior, status and characterized as cowardly, to defeat the Arabs, have their own State, and cause the contraction of the '*abode of Islam*'. All these events contradict the march of History and Allah's design..."

Thus by *fiat* of the Islamic dogma, the assembled Muslim theologians representing the highest Islamic authorities in the entire Muslim world (including most of the non-Arab Muslim countries) arrived at the following determination as summarized by Mr. Green:

> ***"The ideas expounded in this volume (i.e. conference proceedings) could lead to the urge to liquidate Israel (politicide) and the Jews (genocide). If the evil of the Jews is immutable and***

---

[43] The word "Allah" is used instead of "God" by permission of the author.

permanent, transcending time and circumstances, and imper-
vious to all hopes of reform, there is only one way to cleanse
the world of them—by their complete annihilation. Did the
participants of this Conference intend this, and were they
conscious of the dangers concealed in such reasonings? Yet its
inner logic could easily lead to such a conclusion".

But, what was the historical background that led to this conference? The following brief historical note provides the manner of the interplay between the Naksah (setback) characterization of Israel's founding and victories, vs, the theological Nakbah (ultimate catastrophe) characterization of the founding of Israel and subsequent victories.

History of the "Nakbah" and the "Naksah": An illustration of smokescreen politics

To understand the Arab – Israeli crisis one needs to understand two concepts which are encapsulated in the two above mentioned words: Nakbah and Naksah.

Nakbah simply means "a catastrophe".

Naksah means "a setback".

Nakbah is mostly used by the Islamic clergy as they see the very presence of Jews and the State of Israel as a threat and a challenge to the whole edifice of Islam.

In the interim, Naksah was popularized by the late Egyptian President Gamal Abdel Nasser.

Nasser used the term "Naksah" to combat the whole radicalization movement, who challenged his socialistic politics. Nasser explained that it was possible to gain a military victory over the Jews as he kept repeating the mantra, "...whatever is taken by force must be regained by force," in other words the perpetrators and the aggressors will be ousted by force. It was this that enabled and gave him legitimacy before the Arab world to take the aggression case before the UN general assembly.

Naksah ushered in the political engagement with the non- Muslims, as Nasser and his fellow Muslim Arab leaders realized that their legitimacy was slipping away very fast from their hands. Like him, they were also vulnerable; so they hung onto the term, "Naksah" rather than "Nakbah". But their real premise was and continued to be rooted religiously, so they had to interchangeably refer to Nakbah from time to time.

The Western powers including Israel thought that political solutions were and are possible.

The wars of 1948, 1956, and finally after few minor and major skirmishes the 1967 Six Day War sealed the fate of the concept of Naksah, so that even Nasser had to seek the assistance of the clergy to control the rising tide of the Nakbah concept which was gathering momentum in that the answer or true response to the state of Israel was becoming nothing less than a full fledged Jihad and return back to Islam of the 'righteous predecessors' (a'salaf a'saleh'). Hence Nasser ended up calling a conference of all the leading Ulama, the learned Muslim clergy from across the Islamic world in 1968.

It was this 1968 conference, looked upon by the West as irrelevant rhetoric, that actually gave legitimacy to the Nasser regime in the vast majority of the Islamic believing countries, so that in the end their leaders saw the light and were coming round to embrace total Jihad against Israel and not negotiations, or at its worst kept the illusion of negotiations while planning towards the full Jihad.

President Anwar Al Sadat (who came to power in 1970 after the death of Nasser) combined the two concepts brilliantly and proclaimed his personal Islamic identity with the Nakbah position on the one hand, thus gaining the support of the hard liners, while continuing to pursue political remedies through negotiations (a Naksah position) following the October war of 1973.

The Egyptian peace treaty with Israel required official Islamic justification (Fatwa) which was issued and complied with by the Head of the Islamic headship of Al Azhar though very tactfully issued in its ambiguity of terms used—blurring the lines between the Nakbah and Naksah and thus making it acceptable.

However, it is significant to mention that when the decision makers and opinion formers of the Arab and Islamic world met in the Cairo

Conference of 1968 none of them ever mentioned "Naksah" as that was never part of their vocabulary, but they all consolidated the Qur'anic enmity to the Jews as a divine directive in particular and the Islamic position of this Nakbah directive in general.

The same tactic was repeated by late Yasser Arafat when signing Oslo peace treaty referring to it as the equivalent of the Hudeibiya treaty that was signed by Muhammad with the Quraish, which was supposed to last for ten years before being reviewed, however within two years—18 months to be precise, he attacked and Mecca was conquered.[44]

In other words from a political prospective Sadat and the many of the Arab Leaders since Nasser, have played with the dual concept of Naksah and Nakbah subject to the opportunities that would come their way.

As we have earlier established, Hamas, Hizbullah, Al-Qaeda and the government of Iran, will have nothing to do with the Naksah concept, but hold the line that the State of Israel is the Nakbah to Islam and the entire Muslim Ummah and that this catastrophe would not end except with full and total removal or ejection of Israel.

---

[44] http://www.gamla.org.il/english/article/1999/jan/cair3.htm

chapter 4
Jihad Against the Jews: Mandated Enmity[45]

If the Palestinian problem were to be solved would enmity against Israel and the Jews end?

We have established the "enmity" as being an eternal religious doctrine in Islam in the foregoing chapters, but we have not yet drawn the conclusion that this "enmity" is at the root of a wider religious war, and that a religious war has a religious name—Jihad.

Many have misunderstood the revealed enmity as taught in the Qur'an and the Sunnah, and might even be bewildered by the previous section on the eternal validity of this Islamic enmity against the Jews—as they have viewed the Jewish and Christian relationship with Islam and particularly the Jewish-Muslim relations as

> **Implications of the "Muslim Abraham"**
>
> Jewish-Muslim relations are commonly presented in Western thinking as being firmly rooted in the presumed "One Abrahamic faith" of the "People of the Book"...This line of thinking would hold that once the political/land issue is resolved, the Jihad would automatically come to a halt...But is this really the case?

---

[45] Hassan Khaled Mufti of the Lebanese Republic page 63 Arab Theologians on Jews and Israel D.L. Green 1976. Under the title, "Jihad in the Cause of Allah," Sheikh Hassan Khaled makes the summation observation, "Some scholars view that the Muslims who are distant from the battle-field of Palestine such as the Algerians, the Moroccans, all the Africans, Saudi Arabia people, Yemeni people, the Indians, Iraqi people, the Russians and Europeans are indeed sinful if they do not hasten to offer all possible means to achieve success and gain victory in the Islamic battle against their enemies and the enemies of their Religion. Particularly this battle is not a mere combat between two parties, but it is a battle between two religions (namely it is a religious battle). Zionism in fact represents a very perilous cancer, aiming at domineering the Arab countries and the whole Islamic world."

being firmly rooted in the presumed "One Abrahamic faith" of the "People of the Book". Thinking that because the Qur'an makes reference to the patriarchs and the Old Testament prophets, then the assumed logic would be that the enmity must be land-oriented and political rather than theological. This line of thinking would hold that once the political/land issue is resolved, the Jihad would automatically come to a halt.

To be able to comprehend the response to that perspective to be given herein, we first need to explain that according to the Qur'an, Judaism as a religion per se is an innovation , so is Christianity, and therefore both are in violation of that which Allah had originally revealed to the Children of Israel concerning "monotheism."

> ### Use of Veiled Terminologies
>
> By the use of similar, thus apparently "friendly" terminology, with different meanings to obscure and disguise the underlying enmity, Muhammad was able to mount a veiled and virtually undetectable stealth attack on the foundations and tenets of the Jewish and Christian scriptures.

Secondly, in the Qur'an, the Jews and the Christians were and are in reality "Muslims," since all the Jewish patriarchs and prophets including Jesus were themselves "Muslims"—Muslims who allegedly preached Islam from the outset within the Torah, their main purpose being the foretelling of the coming of Muhammad as the "Seal of the Prophets."

In other words all the so called "friendly" Qur'anic terminology, such as the designations as being the "People of the Book," and the "Children of Israel" are all smokescreen terminology which disguised the underlying enmity and enabled Muhammad to put a positive spin on Jews and Christians as "people groups" rather than adherents of established "religions," while denying and dismantling the foundations of their belief systems—Judaism and Christianity.

Thus he was able to mount a veiled and virtually undetectable stealth attack on the foundations and tenets of the Jewish and Christian scriptures.

He achieved that by imposing his views and twisting their scriptures for his own ends to validate his mission, while simultaneously charging or accusing them falsely of corrupting their own scriptures for removing the "prophecies" about his advent "with their "own hands",[46] but without ever producing any evidence. Hence he was able to simultaneously deny their scriptures and still derive his validity, by twisting their text and imposing his reinterpretation of it, declaring it to be speaking of him as their "promised one."[47]

Let's unpack and substantiate the above assertions, starting with the Muslim identity of the Jewish patriarchs and the Jewish prophets as portrayed in the Qur'an and ending with the complete replacement of the foundations of their Judeo-Christian belief system.

Muslims, we all are...! Really...?!!

The Fitrah Doctrine

According to the Islamic doctrine of Fitrah[48] all mankind from eternity has been submitted to Allah and thus all are "Muslims." The Qur'anic argument goes that Allah, having created man, he took a covenant or a pact with mankind, and in so doing, bound everyone to a covenant, that they all will believe in and obey him only, Sura 7:172, *"And (remember) when your Lord brought forth from the Children of Adam, from their loins, their seed (or from Adam's loin his offspring) and made them testify as to themselves (saying): 'Am I not your Lord?' They said: 'Yes! We testify,' lest you should say on the Day of Resurrection: 'Verily, we have been unaware of this.'"*

The term "Covenant" in Islam needs explaining. Just like all other terms, be they theological, social, or political, or whatever, Islam has reinterpreted them all. So the vocabulary/terminology remains the same, however, the concepts and definitions are radically and dramatically different from the general perceived and standard definitions.

As such, Allah making a "covenant with mankind" does not bear the Judeo-Christian understanding of covenant, but more so of a unilateral directive issued by Allah for mankind to uphold.

---

[46] Sura 2:79

[47] Sura 6:20, 2:146 and others

[48] An Islamic concept of nature of a human being which conveys that it is in one's DNA to be Muslim for that is an in-built device by Allah in every human being.

In order not to deviate from the topic we would have to recognize that this is a theological concept of grave socio political implications well beyond the scope of this work. Hence it is sufficient for our limited purposes to state:

1. This 'covenant of Allah' is unilateral and irrevocable,

2. That it remains more of a pact rather than covenant as it is framed in a master–slave relationship,

3. It is and remains non-redemptive should mankind go astray.

In other words, Allah brought out the whole of mankind from the loins of Adam, that is the whole of the human race, asked them and made them testify or make a confession of faith in him against themselves. This means that if their actual state at any point in the future would be inconsistent with what they have covenanted with Allah, then they would be condemned, or that by covenanting, if their actual state would for any reason turn out to be different (i.e. any change of religion for any reason), this original testimony would be held against them. Then Allah reinserted them back into the loins of their forefathers, such that the decision was made and finalized from that point in time, that they would be in full submission to Allah, and should they deviate they would be going against their Allah-given nature and thus would be accountable.

> **"Allah's Covenant"**
>
> The Islamic "covenant of Allah" is not a covenant in the biblical sense, but is instead an ordinance and a directive...a pact imposed by Allah upon mankind...to be obeyed and upheld...framed in a masterslave relationship.

This covenant was twofold. One, it was about the oneness of Allah which is known as **Tawheed,** (which will be further explained below) and the second aspect was the finality of Muhammad as the seal of the Prophets.

The finality of Muhammad and Oneness of Allah are inseparable

Tawheed (misunderstood in English as absolute monotheism), is not monotheism as we know it, but is instead defined as "Islamic Monotheism" and is by definition is inseparable from the finality of Muhammad—

as he simply is not just the "final prophet," but his rights, sanctity, and authority is equal to that of Allah in everything, as stated by the most notable Muslim scholar Ibn Taymiyya[49]. Muslim scholars have established a direct and unbreakable link between the doctrine of Tawheed and the doctrine of Al-Walaa' wa Al-Baraa' (Allegiance and Rejection). In other words, allegiance unto Allah and his messenger must be demonstrated through one's enmity towards the enemies of Allah outwardly and that enmity is to continue forever unless they embrace Islam as per Sura 60:4, "*...we have rejected you, and there has started between us and you, hostility and hatred forever, until you believe in Allâh Alone...*" Clearly, this is a reference to the Jews, but not only the Jews—because as referenced earlier, anyone whose "state" has differed for any reason from the original Allah-given state of being a Muslim has made himself an enemy of Allah, or a "Kafir."

Hence, because of the covenant taken between Allah and the seed of Adam, Islam regards that every human being, when born bears within himself/herself a notion of a faith in Allah and his teachings willingly or unwillingly as a natural part of one's very being or one's DNA. This is the Fitrah, as described earlier.

Sura 3:83, "*Do they seek other than the religion of Allah (the true Islamic Monotheism worshipping none but Allah Alone), while to Him submitted all creatures in the heavens and the earth, willingly or unwillingly. And to Him shall they all be returned.*"

---

[49] Ibn Taymiyyah states in his book "Assaarim wal Maslool 'ala Shaatem Arrasoul, PP 40-41, "Allah's rights and the Messenger's rights are equal and same. The sanctity of Allah is the same as that of Muhammad. Whoever vex the Messenger vex Allah, and whoever obeys the Messenger then he has already obeyed Allah, because the "Ummah" has no connection with their creator except through the Messenger. No one has a means to Allah except through the Messenger, and Allah has substituted Muhammad for Himself in all matters for commanding and forbidding, and revealing. No distinction is allowed to be made between Allah and his Messenger in any of these matters. Ibn Taymiyyah said, "The declaration of faith, 'There is no god but Allah', requires you to love only for the sake of Allah, to hate only for the sake of Allah, to ally yourself only for the sake of Allah, to declare enmity only for the sake of Allah; it requires you to love what Allah loves and to hate what Allah hates. It also requires you to ally yourself to the Muslims wherever you find them and to oppose the disbelievers even if they are your closest kin." (Al-Ihtijaj bi'l-Qadar, p.62).

So this means that every human being is born a Muslim, but it is his family, his community or his environment that perverts him to make him a "non Muslim" such as a Jew, a Christian, or a non believer of any persuasion. Under that definition, Jews and Christians are "converts" who need to be "returned" to Islam, but being born a Muslim is a natural part of one's natural fabric or DNA inherited from one's original parents as a created by Allah.

Muslimhood of all the prophets

Thus we have established that according to the Qur'an, all human beings are born Muslims so this would include prophets and patriarchs— who being born Muslims, they all bowed to Allah in Islam. In so doing, Islam ignores any reference to "Judaism" or "Christianity" as belief systems or "religions" and makes the direct claim that Islam is Allah's "only religion" as established in the Qur'anic quotations below:

- Sura 10:71-72, "*And recite to them the news of Noah...behold he (Noah) said to his people. I have been commanded to be one of the Muslims...*"

- Sura 2:128, "*Abraham/ Ibrahim says...Our Lord! make of us Muslims...*"

- Sura 3:67, "*Ibrahim (Abraham) was neither a Jew nor a Christian, but he was a true Muslim...*"

- Sura 2:133, "*Ismaeel, Isaac and Jacob's offspring will submit to Allah as Muslims...*"

- Sura 12:99, 101, "*Yusuf (Joseph said) 'cause me to die as a Muslim'.*"

- Sura 10:84, "*Musa said: 'O my people! If you have believed in Allâh, then put your trust in Him if you are Muslims'.*"

- Sura 3:52, "*...disciples of Jesus Then when 'Iesa (Jesus) came to know of their disbelief, he said: "Who will be my helpers in Allah's Cause?" the disciples said: 'We are the helpers of Allah; we believe in Allah, and bear witness that we are Muslims'.*"

- Sura 5:111, *"And when I (Allâh) put in the hearts of the disciples [of Jesus] to believe in Me and My Messenger, they said: 'We believe. And bear witness that we are Muslims.'"*

- Suras 2:136, 3:84, *"...all the prophets were Muslims with Allah's confirmation..."*

- Sura 3:84, *"Say (O Muslims), "We believe in Allah and that which has been sent down to us and that which has been sent down to Ibrahim, Ishmael, Isaac, Jacob, and to[the twelve sons of Jacob, and that which has been given to Moses and 'Iesa (Jesus), and that which has been given to the Prophets from their Lord. We make no distinction between any of them, and to Him we have submitted and are Muslims."*

- Sura 3:85, *"And whoever seeks a religion other than Islâm, it will never be accepted of him, and in the Hereafter he will be one of the losers..."*

- Sura 3:19, *"Truly, the religion with Allâh is Islâm...."*

All of the prophets being Muslims, preaching and proclaiming the religion of Allah — Islam, the source of what they were given was the eternal tablet. According to Islam everything and anything that was important and relevant was incorporated from these previous scriptures into the Qur'an as the final revelation, (see fig. 1). As all of these previous books, including the Old and New Testaments, have been tampered with by its followers, Allah has abrogated them upon the arrival of the Qur'an.

> ## Mohammad coached by Muslim Prophet Musa (Moses) during "Night Journey" regarding the number of daily Muslim prayers
>
> Starting with Allah's command of 50 daily prayers, Musa advised Muhammad, *"What did your Lord enjoin on your Ummah' I (Muhammad) said, 'Fifty prayers everyday and night.' He said, 'Go back to your Lord and ask Him to reduce (the burden) for your Ummah, for your Ummah will not be able to do that."* After many iterations back and forth between Musa and Allah, the number came down to 5 prayers, at which point Musa advised of a lower number, but Muhammad said, *"I had kept going back to my Lord until I felt too shy."*
>
> (See Chapter 6 for details of the Night Journey).

So the foregoing references make it clear that all the prophets were Muslims and were sent to preach Islam, i.e. not to establish any other faith or religious system such as Judaism or Christianity. In this regard, the early revelations were given to so-called "Muslim Patriarchs, and prophets", not to Jewish Patriarchs nor to Christian Apostles—and thus they were always proclaiming the religion of Islam.

As will be demonstrated in Chapter 6, Muhammad's later "Night Journey" vision/dream vividly pictures this Qur'anic doctrine (among others) of the "Muslimhood" aspect of all of the prophets—as Muhammad allegedly communes and prays with all the prophets enroute to the presence of Allah in the highest heavens. In one instance, "Muslim prophet Musa" (Moses) advises Muhammad regarding the number of daily ritual prayers for the Muslim Ummah. (See box above)

Those who have failed to understand the foregoing and its implications according to the Islamic Jurisprudence, keep on referring to the Sura 5:20-21, as land apportioned by Allah to the Jews, as the right of the Jews attested by the Qur'an.

Sura 5: 20-21, "*20 And (remember) when Moses said to his people: "O my people! Remember the Favour of Allah to you, when He made Prophets among you, made you kings, and gave you what He had not given to any other among the worlds in the past." 21 "O my people! Enter the holy land which Allah has assigned to you, and turn not back (in flight) for then you will be returned as losers.*"

We have already explained in the foregoing that the Muslimhood of all the prophets and the Jews means they were followers of Islam which was proclaimed by Moses. The land itself was given by Allah and not a different deity as claimed by the Jews. As all the subsequent prophets and the kings of the Jews were Muslims and portrayed as such, the present day Jews are usurpers and not the rightful owners of the land.

But Jews are neither Muslims nor are they followers of their prophets who preached Islam.

Allah's pact or "covenant" with the prophets

Secondly, Allah's pact with mankind was not limited only to the one-god concept, or Oneness of Allah as is commonly thought, but more importantly that Muhammad as his prophet completes the Islamic Tawheed, i.e. Allah and Muhammad are inextricably linked. But this second part according to the Qur'an was revealed only to "the prophets to be." Those Prophets were spoken to by Allah in advance, told of the coming of Muhammad and were required to agree that they would make Muhammad known to their followers and to expect his arrival in the future, as per Sura 3:81. In other words, Abraham, and all the prophets had already taken an alleged covenant from Allah to proclaim the coming of Muhammad.[50]

> **Predictions of Muhammad's Coming**
>
> The "Muslim patriarchs" of the Biblical scriptures were told by Allah of Muhammad's coming, as documented in Sura 3:81, and were then instructed to predict him, proclaim him, and upon his arrival, help him carry out his mission as "Seal of the Prophets."

Sura 3:81, *"And (remember) when Allah took the Covenant of the Prophets, saying: "Take whatever I gave you from the Book and understanding of the Laws of Allah, and afterwards there will come to you a Messenger (Muhammad) confirming what is with you; you must, then, believe in him and help him." Allah said: "Do you agree (to it) and will you take up My Covenant (which I conclude with you)?" They said: "We agree." He said: "Then bear witness; and I am with you among the witnesses (for this)."* (Q_Al-Hilali)

Sura 33:7, *"And (remember) when We took from the Prophets their covenant, and from you (O Muhammad SAW), and from Nûh (Noah), Ibrâhîm (Abraham), Mûsa (Moses), and 'Iesa (Jesus), son of Maryam (Mary). We took from them a strong covenant."*

---

[50] More details about the supremacy of Muhammad from purely Islamic authoritative sources are provided in Appendices, D, E and F.

The Anchor prophets

These five Prophets (Muhammad, Noah, Abraham, Moses and Jesus) are known as the "Anchor Prophets" (Ulul—Uzm, in Arabic) in the Qur'an. As a group they have a higher status than the rest of the Prophets although among this group some are more elevated than others, with Muhammad being at the highest level. They each presumably started a new school or dispensation, with each given a "Shariah" for their time, limited only to the people they were sent to, again with the exception of Muhammad—who is said to have brought the final and eternal Shariah to all mankind and all creation. Therefore, all previous Shariah's are now abrogated and replaced by the Islamic Shariah—hence Muhammad is the best of Anchor Prophets, being the alleged "Seal of the Prophets".[51]

Thus according to the Qur'an the prophecy of Muhammad's coming as the final prophet allegedly within the Torah and the Gospels is regarded as the most important part of their respective messages, so that their prophetic proclamations would have included his detailed description and mission so that when he, Muhammad, would arrive, the people of his day would immediately recognize him as the one that "was to come."

So according to the Qur'an the Muslim "prophet" Isa (Jesus) foretold of a prophet who was yet to come, giving his name, as per Sura 61:6. This alleged glad tidings is reported in the Qur'an to have been given to the Jews bearing confirmation of their previous revelations, thus establishing that the coming of this "Ahmad" was already mentioned in their scriptures:

Sura 61:6, *"And (remember) when 'Iesa (Jesus), son of Maryam (Mary), said: "O Children of Israel! I am the Messenger of Allah unto you confirming the Torah which came before me, and giving glad tidings of a Messenger to come after me, whose name shall be Ahmad."*

Not only the Muslim Isa (i.e. Jesus) announced Muhammad's coming but he, Muhammad, was the central theme of the previous scriptures, so claims the Qur'an that the central prophecy of the Law (Torah) and the Gospel (New Testament) was the unlettered (illiterate) Prophet:

---

[51] See Appendix F describing the highest level prophets called in Arabic "Ulul-Uzm". This is available in a Fatwa at: http://islamqa.com/en/ref/7459/bayt%20al%20maqdis

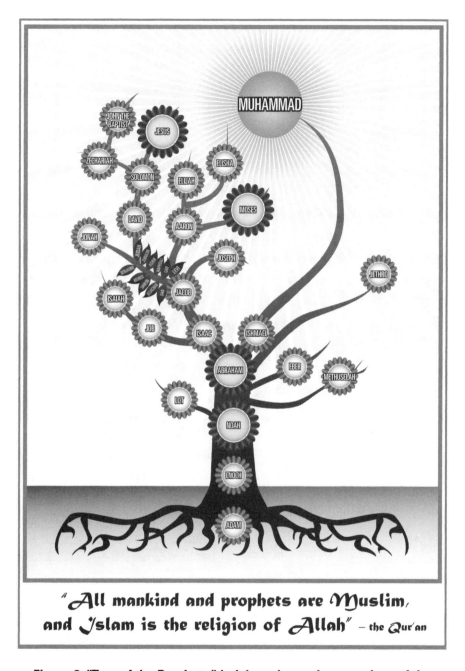

"All mankind and prophets are Muslim, and Islam is the religion of Allah" – the Qur'an

Figure 3: "Tree of the Prophets," in Islam shows the genealogy of the "prophets" starting with Adam and ending with Muhammad through the Ishmael line.

Sura 7:157, *"Those who follow the messenger, the unlettered Prophet, whom they find mentioned in their own (scriptures),- in the law and the Gospel; for he (Muhammad) commands them virtue and forbids from vice; he (Muhammad) allows them as lawful what is good (and pure) and prohibits them from what is bad (and impure); He (Muhammad) releases them from their heavy burdens and from the yokes that are upon them. So it is those who believe in him (Muhammad), honour him, help him, and follow the light which is sent down with him,- it is they who will prosper."*

Sura 4:80, *"Whosoever obeys the Apostle (Muhammad) has already obeyed Allah…"*

Sura 6:20, *"Those to whom We have given the Scripture (Jews and Christians) recognize him (i.e. Muhammad) as they recognize their own sons…"*

Sura 2:146, *"Those to whom We gave the Scripture (Jews and Christians) recognise him (Muhammad) as they recognise their sons. But verily, a party of them conceal the truth while they know it."*

As such, Islam according to Muslims, isn't an ideology that Muhammad came up with, but it is part and parcel of every living human being as created by Allah. This belief is based on the Islamic doctrine of Fitra. As explained earlier, Fitra means, natural or what comes naturally, or comes into being naturally. Sura 30:30 explains it, *"So set your face towards the religion of pure Islamic Monotheism (Allah's Fitrah), according to which He has created mankind."*

> ### Significance of the "Muslimhood" of all creation
> Since there is no Judaism or Christianity per se, the Jews and Christians are guilty of deviating from the "true path"…Therefore they must be fought against, and be brought into the supposed "fold of Allah."

Hence in reality there is nothing called Judaism or Christianity in the Qur'an, since all past generations were Muslims including the Jews and Christians, except that they had rebelled, just as the present generation is still in rebellion against Allah and his apostle, Muhammad.

However the Qur'an points out that it is the Jews in particular who perverted the way, changed their scriptures, and continue to oppose and persecute those who want to follow Muhammad—as they were the main custodians of most of the revelations from Allah, though through their allegedly "Muslim" patriarchs. But the Qur'an reports that when Muhammad did come, they—the Jews—refused to recognize him, and then perverted and corrupted their own scriptures to remove the predictions of his coming. Hence they are the permanent enemy of Islam, Muhammad, and the Muslim Ummah, and as such, are charged of having misled the whole of humanity, according to Islamic beliefs.

Consequently, the Qu'ran holds that because the Jews and the Christians have not followed the true path, they are not fighting for the cause of Allah but for Satan.

One might ask, how do they—the Jews and Christians—fight for the cause of Satan? The Qur'an says: By corrupting their scriptures, by refusing to acknowledge the final messenger whom their scriptures had predicted, and by commanding vice and forbidding virtue, rather than the opposite. Therefore they must be fought against, and be brought into the supposed "fold of Allah."

There are, of course, tens of verses on these issues, but let's just quote two:

Sura 4:76 *"Those who believe fight in the Cause of Allah, and those who disbelieve fight in the cause of Satan, So fight you against the friends of (Satan); Ever feeble indeed is the plot of Satan."*

Sura 2:257, *"Allah is the Protector or Guardian of those who believe. He brings them out from darkness into light. But as for those who disbelieve, their Auliyia (supporters and helpers) are Taghutt [false deities and false leaders, etc.], they bring them out from light into darkness. Those are the dwellers of the Fire, and they will abide therein forever."*

When Allah desired to restore mankind to his fold (Islamic monotheism, Tawheed) to serve Him alone even though the polytheists detest it, he prepared his final and his best prophet for this most important divine mission, namely Muhammad.

Sura 48:28, " *He it is Who has sent His Messenger (Muhammad) with guidance and the religion of truth (Islam), that He may make it (Islam) superior over all religion. And All-Sufficient is Allah as a Witness.*"

Islamic Mission Call: The Da'wa

A call or an ultimatum?

Hence, to bring them back to his fold, Allah has devised a method. This method has been made obligatory on all Muslims to participate in any form or shape they can, such as: with their tongue, their finances, with themselves, with migrations and volunteering to go to the battlefield to engage the enemy physically. This method is named in Islam as, "Jihad." Allah has prescribed Jihad.[52] So it is of paramount importance to note that Jihad is part of Da'wa, Islamic mission call. As Jihad and its doctrine is a topic of its own, we won't get involved in the full spectrum of Jihad and its details, such as defensive Jihad and offensive Jihad and its sub-divisions.

> **Bringing "Back" to the Islamic Fold**
>
> The issuing of the Da'wa "call" is tacitly but explicitly backed up with a method: Jihad. By refusing this call, one is "assumed" to be at war with Islam. Hence Jihad is always defensive.

Instead, we need to focus and state that Jihad in all of its forms is there to aid Islamic missions for the reversion (conversion) of people and to bring them back to Allah's fold voluntarily or by force. So Jihad is an integral and indispensable part of the "Da'wa," the Islamic "Call," i.e. the call to embrace Islam. It's clear, once one has been given an invitation, i.e. the

---

[52] Sheikh Abdullah Ghoshah Supreme Judge Hashemite Kingdom of Jordan/ Arab Theologians on Jews and Israel D. L. Green 1976. In his article, "The Jihad Is the Way to Gain Victory," Sheikh Abdullah Ghoshah gives an outline of the Islamic doctrine of Jihad, and the conditions under which the Ummah is obligated to carry it out by all means, military and otherwise. He then makes the observation, "Treachery was the business of Jews throughout their ages and times as it was their instinct to break their covenant with others and resort to treachery as soon as they had any chance to betray others…" In the previous paragraph he would state quite interestingly, "The Muslims are also free to break their covenant with the enemies if they are uneasy lest the enemies should betray them."

Call, and it is refused, then one must be subjected to forceful means, although as we shall see, this Jihad is always presented as defensive in nature. The Qur'an has clearly stated the objective of this Jihad in Sura 9:33, *"It is He Who has sent His Messenger (Muhammad) with guidance and the religion of truth (Islam), to make it superior over all religion even though the polytheists, hate (it)."*

Hence Jihad is always viewed by Muslims as ***defensive***.

One might ask the obvious question, that once a sword is lifted against unarmed people, how can it remain defensive?

From an Islamic point of view, no matter how brutal Jihad may be, it is always defensive in nature and never an aggression, for the real aggressors are always the unbelievers (chiefly the Jews) who have vexed the prophet and his master by rejecting his mission and his message—this rejection is initiated and headed by the Jews. This rejection of the invitation to embrace Islam is in itself a heinous crime which falls under the doctrine of "Fitnah" or "Dissension."

> ### The Key Purpose and Justification of Jihad
>
> Jihad is considered the only mechanism to return and restore mankind to Allah's fold. In other words, for a Muslim, it isn't proclamation like the Christian Gospel where response is left to the free will of the recipient, with judgement left to the divine being at the end. Jihad executes judgement here and now.

Hence the soldiers of Allah are justified in waging every form of Jihad against the transgressors.

Sura 8:39, *"And fight them until there is no more Fitnah (sedition or dissenion) (disbelief and polytheism: i.e. worshipping others besides Allah) and the religion (worship) will all be for Allah Alone [in the whole of the world]. But if they cease (worshipping others besides Allah), then certainly, Allah is All-Seer of what they do."*

Sura 9:29, *"Fight against those who (1) believe not in Allah, (2) nor in the Last Day, (3) nor forbid that which has been forbidden by Allah and His Messenger (4) and those who acknowledge not the religion of truth (i.e. Islam) among the people of the Scripture (Jews and Chris-*

tians), until they pay the Jizyah with willing submission, and feel themselves subdued."

Returning mankind back to Allah's fold

This is why from an Islamic point of view, Jihad is considered the only mechanism to return and restore mankind to Allah's fold, in other words, for a Muslim, it isn't a proclamation like that of a Christian Gospel aimed at the free will of the recipient, with judgement left to the divine being at the end, but is now and here. It is the very actualization of forcing people into the fold of Allah. Should they reject it, then the very mechanism which was meant to bring them into the fold could in turn see the end of the "inviter," for it is possible that the "invitee" may use force against force, therefore the inviter may be killed in battle. What we see as "terrorism" is nothing less than a mechanism to save one or the other side or maybe both, should the "invitee" respond positively to Islam.

That is why a "martyr" has privileges and his immediate family treat him as a hero. He is not mourned for—it is a celebration, for he has obtained favour at the highest levels, with the possibility, some Islamic scholars say, that he or she may have the right to petition for 10 closest loved ones.

Therefore the only mechanism to provide "salvation" to mankind according to Islam, is Jihad. It may seem counterintuitive to the uninitiated to consider the remote possibility that Jihad in any way could provide "salvation." However, what we are showing is that in returning non-Muslims to the Islamic fold they have been saved from rebelling against Allah.

Just as fasting and prayer are prescribed and obligatory as in Sura 2:183," *O you who believe! fasting is prescribed for you as it was prescribed for those before you,*" Jihad as well is prescribed. Equally like fasting and praying, all forms of activities leading to violent Jihad remains a religious obligation imposed by divine will on all Muslims forever until the day of resurrection—even though they (the Muslims) may not like it, hence they have no choice.

Sura 2:216, "*Jihad (holy fighting in Allah's Cause) is ordained for you (Muslims) though you dislike it, and it may be that you dislike a thing which is good for you and that you like a thing which is bad for you. Allah knows but you do not know."*

Jihad can only cease when the whole earth has been Islamized and all its inhabitants have embraced Islam—the Jews being the worst aggressors! The Jews are the biggest blockage, the worst enemies of Muhammad, and the worst offenders against Allah and the Muslim community and those who would want to accept the path of Allah as revealed to Muhammad. Therefore, not only must they be fought against relentlessly, but must be fully eliminated and annihilated.

Because of this, Muslims are required not to enter into permanent peace with the enemies of Allah or else Jihad would have to be suspended, thus resulting in disobedience to Allah and his messenger. That's why the Jihadi movements such as Hamas or the Islamic Jihad agree only to a temporary cease fire or truce with Israel (known as "Hudna"), and not to any form of a permanent peace agreement, lest they suspend the binding Jihad obligation, and find themselves in disobedience to Allah and his messenger, Muhammad. *"For whosoever obeys the Messenger has already obeyed Allah…"* according to Sura 4:80. For an example of this type of "truce" see the footnote below[53] and the Treaty of Hudaybiah as described at the end of Chapter 3.

Naturally Muslims would say that Jihad was first prescribed because of persecution and injustices against Muslims, as per Sura 22:39, *"To those against whom war is made, permission is given to fight, because they are wronged;- and verily, Allah is most powerful for their aid."*

But note the phraseology "To those against whom war is made…", as it sounds as if it means that if attacked physically, as in military aggression, there is the "right to defend"—but this depends on the definition of the word "attack" as used in the Qur'an and Islamic source books. In the West the word "attack" is universally understood as a physical aggression, or open declaration of "war" rather even than threats—although the practice of informed "pre-emptive strikes" with sufficient evidence, is increasingly applied. But in Islam, the word "attack" is defined categorically to include

---

[53] http://www.gamla.org.il/english/article/1999/jan/cair3.htm

ANY opposition, criticism, passive or active, intended or unintended against Islam as a "religion" or perceived insults against Muhammad, or any presence or influence of non-Muslims within a Muslim society[54]. In other words, one can be "at war with Islam" without even knowing it!!!

How is this convoluted logic possible—and how is it applied?

Assumed Enmity in Defence of Islam

As explained earlier, the outcome of the covenant made by Allah with the children of Adam in reality means Allah does not and will not tolerate any form of opposition. Any opposition which would contain a notion of doubt or mockery even though unintentional will be severely dealt with. This is why Muhammad dealt most severely and brutally with his critics in his day naming this criticism as enmity, dissenion, and ultimately as threat to the welfare of the Islamic state and the Muslim community. Whether it was meant or not on Muhammad's part, it was understood and perceived as an "assumed hostility or enmity," as though it were real. Therefore, making war on Islam means any form of resisting or criticising any tenet of Islam or the person of Muhammad, even if that criticism is a historically documented fact—as categorically stated by Qadi Ayyad, a renowned Islamic scholar, in his book "A'shifa fi Huquq al Mustapha". Truth is therefore not a defence, but is sufficient reason and occasion for defensive retaliation.

A cover for "offence" in the name of "defence"

In other words it's always only defensive from the Islamic point of view. Consequently, as we have already explained, that as non-Muslim mankind is in a state of enmity with Allah and his messenger, therefore they are reckoned to be the aggressors.

> **Assumed Enmity: Any Criticism, or the Refusal to Accept the Islamic Call**
>
> This concept was developed and implemented by Muhammad in Medina, thus establishing a mechanism for maintaining a perpetual defensive stance for Jihad.

---

[54] As explained by Qadi Ayyad in his classic book, "Huquq Al-Mustafa" (The Rights of the Chosen One, Muhammad)

Thus any Jihad undertaken against non-Muslims is considered to be defensive, though doctrinally there are various names and titles given to different kinds of Jihad though in the end its aim is either to get rid of the enemies of Allah (which we have identified) or effectively to Islamize them and the rest of the world. Therefore, a discussion of what people consider "the spectrums" of Jihad from the inner struggle to the sword is beside the point and will not be dealt with in this treatise.

Islam began in what is known presently as Saudi Arabia, but how did it reach Egypt, Libya, Tunis, Morocco, Algeria, and elsewhere? Did it reach to these places through peaceful means, and civilized dialogue?

Were the conquering armies religious learned men, who proclaimed their message peacefully, or were they composed of hoards of brutal assassins? Were they those who forced their victims to either embrace Islam or die or reduced them to virtual slave status?

If true, when will Jihad end?

With this in mind, one has to ask the following questions:

- Can the concept of world peace and the continuous obligation of Jihad until the day of resurrection go hand in hand?
- If we were to suppose that the economical, social and political injustices were sorted or resolved, the Palestinian conflict were to be justly resolved, Iraq was liberated etc., etc, would this mean that the obligation of Jihad would be suspended or cancelled?
- So if the real objective of Jihad was defensive as claimed by some does that mean that Jihad would be abolished once the attacks on the Muslim community ceases?
- Why was Jihad prescribed? Was it prescribed only to ward off attacks on Muslims? Or are there objectives other than the attacks on the Muslims communities?
- If a country, say UK or France, were to forbid Muslim missionaries from propagating Islamic teaching what would be the Islamic Juristic verdict or reaction be to such a proposition?

- Or, does Jihad continue until the whole world has been Islamised and every living human being has embraced Islam as a religion and a political system?

- If there were no Jihad verses in the Qur'an commanding the Muslims to kill, would the world have witnessed such genocides that continue to take place in the name of Islam?

Iran is an Islamic state that enforces the Shariah and believes in the Qur'an, which commends and commands the Muslims to prepare against its enemies amongst whom are the Jews. The Qur'an teaches them to make ample preparation to strike terror in the hearts of their enemies as per Sura 8:60, "*And make ready against them all you can of power, including steeds of war (tanks, planes, missiles, artillery, etc.) to threaten the enemy of Allah and your enemy, and others besides whom, you may not know but whom Allah does know. And whatever you shall spend in the Cause of Allah shall be repaid unto you, and you shall not be treated unjustly*." Is Islamic Iran's effort trying to produce nuclear weapon in line and obedience to Sura 8:60?

Based on the foregoing, if the Islamic Iran were to possess nuclear weapons does that mean that Iran may create another holocaust against the Jews, especially if Iran were to become superior in military strength to the Jewish state?

Or generally speaking considering the foregoing, what would be the fate of the Jews if the Arab states became stronger than the Israel?

Re-Definition of the Crisis

Having established a few key principles and background factors that are vital components to understanding and having a handle on the question before us, it has been clearly illustrated that rather than an Arab-Israeli, or a Palestinian-Israeli crisis, in reality it is more of a Muslim-Jewish crisis.

In the process we have explained the Muslimhood of the whole human race, and the Muslim identity of all the Jewish patriarchs and Jewish prophets including the Muslim Jesus—whose sole mission was to proclaim Muhammad's coming.

Furthermore, we have clearly established with ample Qur'anic references the root and the origins of Muslim enmity towards the Jews as a divinely revealed command of Allah. Therefore this enmity is here to stay. It is correctly deduced from the primary Islamic sources that Allah himself is against the Jews and is permanently at war with them through the Muslims.

We have outlined tens of Qur'anic references declaring it's almost absolute disdain of the Jews as a repeated and a recurring theme throughout the Qur'an, Sunnah and other sacred manuals of Islam. Added to what we have already stated, even the elements of nature are at war with the Jews, as Allah will command the rocks and trees to cry out at the end of time, *"O Muslim, O slave of Allah, there is a Jew hiding behind me come and slaughter him."*[55]

The foregoing arguments and substantiating texts from the Qur'an and the Hadith have established conclusively that the dispute isn't land-centred, and that the Arab-Israeli crisis isn't just a political crisis. We started out to dispel the myth of the land-centred/political cause for the Arab-Israeli crisis and we have established that the roots are much deeper to the point of revealing the eternal enmity of Islam toward the Jews (and Christians).

In short, this crisis is as old as Islam, and will continue as long as there are Jews and Muslims on this planet, as is affirmed by Al Qaradawi in his recent statement, *"...and it is a duty of the faithful to obey Allah and his apostle and liquidate the enemies of Allah and in particular ...who else but the Jews!"*

Therefore the cessation of Jihad is being addressed as social injustices and every attempt is being made to resolve it through negotiations. But, just like "enmity," it remains neither solvable nor subject to any form of human reforms.

In conclusion to the question that we have been considering, would Jihad cease if the Palestinian crisis were resolved—the answer is a resounding NO, as Jihad against the Jews is an Islamic duty irrespective of the occupation or not.

---

[55] Sahih Muslim book 41, no. 6985

chapter 5
The Outworking: How Muhammad Institutionalized Enmity

The Jews of Arabia prior to Islam

Having established from the pages of the Qur'an, the Hadith, and the current Islamic authorities that the so-called "Arab-Israeli" conflict is not rooted solely in the land, but instead in Allah's enmity toward the Jews as expressed within those Islamic sources since Islam was established— we will now set the social and religious context by going back before the time of Muhammad to show the history of the Jews in Arabia before Islam and the conflict that arose when Muhammad announced his new religion in Mecca.

> **Arab Jews: Outsiders or an Indigenous Arabian Community?**
>
> History testifies that the Jews of Arabia lived as vibrant communities with major contributions to Arab society centuries before Islam came on the scene.

The question here to keep in mind, during a discussion of this period is: What was the relationship of the Arab Jew to others within Arabia prior to the advent of Islam?

There are historians who believe that the earliest Jewish migration to Arabia was under Joshua who had come to pursue the Amalekites. Others have stated later migration during the time of the Babylonian conquest of Israel. It is believed that the Jews who had escaped the siege of Nebuchadnezzar around 589 B.C. had fled and had come to Arabia. They settled in various locations and spread out, building and developing the land. They built major settlements in the oases of Khyber, Wadi Al Qura, Teema, Fadek, Hunain, Ta'if, and beyond, even in Mecca. They influenced the Arabic language, brought in new religious concepts among the Pagan Arabs, many of whom accepted Judaism. Some of those Arabs were later Christianized. Besides developing the various oases, the Jews congregated in large numbers in a city which they founded which they called Yathrib. In that city, three major Jewish clans put their roots down: Banu Nadir, Banu Kaynuka and Banu Qurayza. These three clans would figure strongly in the developments to follow—as their city would become the staging ground for Muhammad's development of the Islamic state.

Leadership vacuum in Yathrib on the eve of Hijra

Long after the Jews settled in Yathrib (later called Medina) the (then-pagan) Arabian Aws[56] and the Khazraj tribes arrived. Historians agree that the Aws and Khazraj were tribes from Qahtan from the Yemen who had to leave their homes as result of the destruction of Marib dam in the 6th century, AD.[57]

The tribal hostilities between the Aws and the Khazraj are recorded in history, their tribal wars continued some 120 years. Their last war had ended just five years before the Hijra, Muhammad's immigration to Yathrib/Medina.

When the Arab tribes arrived in Yathrib, they liked the land which had a number of natural water fountains, and was much more fertile than what they had left behind. They found the majority of the inhabitants were Jews who were in need of manual labourers to work in some of their farms. So they located between Al Hura al Sharkiya and Kuba. Over a period of time they became land owners and developed their own farms and were now wealthy and had built houses all over Yathrib.

Once they were wealthy, there arose a competition/rivalry between them and the Jews over the city's leadership. Individually both the Aws and the Khazraj tribes tried to form separate alliances with the Jews.[58]

---

[56] Sometimes spelt Aus

[57] http://en.wikipedia.org/wiki/Marib_Dam

[58] http://www.exmuslim.com/books/files/religion.pdf

The Jews on their part saw this as their opportunity to regain back their control and to avert a looming danger just in case these new immigrant warring Arab tribes were to unite their forces against them. So the Jews decided to make separate alliances. Hence Banu Nadir and Banu Qurayza made an alliance with the Aws and the Banu Kaynuka with the Khazraj.

As a result of their rivalries there was no real headship or centralized government in Yathrib, hence rivalry continued and overall neither the Jews nor the Arab tribes of Aws and Khazraj were fully satisfied with the outcome.

Further factors prepare the grounds for the Hijra

On the other hand there was yet another rivalry from outside Yathrib that affected them all, namely, from the Quraish tribe in Mecca. After the digging up and restoration of Zamzam (a well in Mecca), the caravans then preferred to travel directly to Mecca rather than divert and stop for water and other supplies in Yathrib as they had done for generations. The newly restored well had given the Quraish an upper hand commercially and religiously as they were the guardians and custodians of the Ka'aba, the place of pilgrimage. The Jews of Yathrib had good relations with the Quraish, but the Aws and Khazraj were anxious to break the Quraish's commercial as well as religious monopoly. This underlying difference in loyalties was fertile ground for Muhammad to exploit as he was already in mortal conflict with the Quraish.

All of these factors led to the immigration of Muhammad to Yathrib. As it turned out the immigration of Muhammad ended up regarded by historians as the most instrumental and decisive event in the struggle between the Arab pagans and the Muslims in Mecca and between the Jews and their Arab allies in Yathrib (Medina). For Muhammad's immigration transformed the weak and insignificant follower Muslim community of Mecca into a powerful and effective force, and forged them into a unified force wherein they would become carriers of new concepts and doctrines.

Failed Immigration Experience Leads to Further Planning

In 620A.D. with the death of Khadija his first wife and Abu Talib his uncle, Muhammad's vulnerability increased as the Quraish were free from all assurances made under tribal law that they had given not to attack him.[59]

At that point the Quraish did plan to Kill him as per Sura 8:30, "*And (remember) when the disbelievers plotted against you (O Muhammad) to imprison you, or to kill you, or to get you out (from Mecca); they were plotting and Allah too was plotting, and Allah is the Best of the plotters.*"

So at this point, the Quraish were considering one of the three options against Muhammad: imprisonment, murder or exile.

As reported by Ibn Ishaq, when Abu Talib died, the Quraish unleashed an unprecedented attack and persecution on Muhammad—so much so, that he was forced to flee to nearby Taif seeking refuge and protection from the Thakif/Sakif[60] clan as he had some close relatives among them. Muhammad, accompanied by his adopted son, Zaid ibn Harith left for Taif seeking to be aided to victory by its Jews and Arabs, only to be hounded and chased out of their town by being stoned and booed.[61] Having been rejected by Thakif of Taif he had nowhere to go but back to Mecca, so he now sought the protection of Mu't'am bin Adi one of the notables of Mecca and a member of the board of its elders.[62]

As a result of this very painful and unexpected rebuff in Taif, his plans to immigrate to Yathrib (Medina) were no longer sudden, as they had been to Taif, as he now had gained time to plan more carefully. This time, he planned meticulously with great care taking note of the most minute of details, which took him two years from 620-622 A.D. as reported in the Sira (biography of Muhammad).

As stated earlier there were two major pagan Arab tribes in Medina /Yathrib, the Aws and Khazraj. Amongst the Khazraj were Banu Najjar, who were related to him from his mother's side as well as his paternal grandfa-

---

[59] Muhammad had used existing tribal customs for protection under his uncle, who was actually a pagan.

[60] http://www.al-eman.com/Islamlib/viewchp.asp?BID=249&CID=28

[61] محمد رسول الله، لمحمد رشيد رضا pages 113-114

[62] *Al Hijra: The Islamic Doctrine of Immigration* by S Solomon & E Al Maqdisi pages 65ff

ther Abdul Muttalib. Since neither his preaching nor the efforts of the Muslim community in Mecca were very effective, he needed a more conducive environment to regroup and grow the community in order to be able to stand against and ultimately defeat his Meccan pagan enemies. Yathrib seemed to offer that opportunity, politically, socially, and religiously.

However, because of the disastrous Ta'if experience, he did not rush into another attempted immigration, but instead took two years to methodically plan the transition—thus his migration to Yathrib had a defined strategy with clear goals to establish an Islamic entity and to eventually avenge the Quraish and the rest of the Meccan pagan tribes.

Muhammad's Relationship with the Jews Prior to Migration

At this point in Muhammad's Meccan era (around 620-622 AD), he strategically showed a favourable face to the Jews and the Christians, i.e. proclaiming that, "we all worship the same God, etc." As we shall see below, this apparent favourable face was clearly a mere show—as the evidence is overwhelming in pointing out that Muhammad never intended to buy into either Judaism or Christianity. He wanted to replace them by claiming that Islam actually preceded them and that, in the final analysis, he was just the last Messenger to set the record straight! Note, for example Sura 3:67, "*Ibrâhim (Abraham) was neither a Jew nor a Christian, but he was a true Muslim…*" However, it is clear from the record that the Jews in Mecca and Medina believed that, at least, Muhammad was a monotheist, had borrowed and thus affirmed a lot of their rules and regulations, and as a result he could be at least, a harmless ally. However, they never thought or considered that he was the final messenger, except of course for those Jews who converted to Islam and provided Muhammad with valuable data on the Bible and the Jews, in general.

Muhammad had realised through his political shrewdness before ever reaching Yathrib that the Jews had a huge potential that he could deploy and benefit from for his cause, due to their supremacy in all aspects: religiously , economically, politically, intellectually, and socially. Also he was aware that in claiming the origin of monotheism he would have to either gain their support or counter their witness in order to retain the authority of their scriptures to back his claims. Therefore, it is obvious that he clearly saw both the advantages and the dangers to his mission as posed by the Jewish tribes.

So though he had spelled out his decision which sealed and settled the fate of the Jews long before he ever reached Yathrib, we see him making a public pretence of getting close to them and befriending them, for nearly a year prior to his actual migration to Medina, and also for a period of time afterwards.

"Revelations" from Mecca increasingly favourable to Jews

For nearly a year before immigration all his new Meccan revelations were more and more affirming of the Jews and harsher and harsher towards the Quraish. He began to incorporate modified versions of the Jewish Patriarchs of Ibrahim (Abraham), Jacob, Joseph, Moses, Aaron, and of Children of Israel.

Such texts as Sura 45:16 "*And indeed We gave the Children of Israel the Scripture, and the understanding of the Scripture and its laws, and the Prophet hood; and provided them with good things, and preferred them above the worlds*," influenced the Jews of Yathrib to add their voice welcoming him as a potential ally. Other pronouncements along those lines include:

- Sura 17:2, "*And We gave Mûsa (Moses) the Scripture and made it guidance for the Children of Israel.*"

- Sura 2:47, "*O Children of Israel! Remember My Favour which I bestowed upon you and that I preferred you above the rest.*"

Little did they know that he was able to abrogate all of his revelations, and make them void.

Pledges of Aqaba

In 620 A.D. while presenting himself to various Arab tribes who were on pilgrimage at Mecca Muhammad came across six men of Aws from Yathrib at Aqaba (a glen between Mecca and Mina). These six had come to make a pact with the Quraish against the Khazraj. According to the Sira of Ibn Hisham, "I was told by Al Hussein ibn Abdel Rahman bin Omar bin Sa'ad bin Ma'az from Mahmoud bin Labid who said when Abu Al Haseer Unsi bani Ra'fa approached Mecca accompanied by men of Bani Abdel Ashhal amongst who was Ayas bin Ma'az seeking a pact with Quraish against the Khazraj, the Apostle of Allah heard of them, came, sat down and asked, have you seen good for which you came for?"[63] In essence, Muhammad was probing to discover if they had made any progress in their mission to make an agreement with the Quraish and inferring that he had a better alternative.

The following year 621 A.D. the same six came back accompanied by another six men from Khazraj, so altogether were 12 (twelve), one of them was a relative of Muhammad. Those six were community leaders known as captains who were like modern day social workers who would know the community well and its needs. Muhammad invited them to embrace Islam, and they pledged their allegiance to him asking them to abstain from overt debauchery. This was the *first Pledge of Aqaba*.

In 622 A.D. some 74 or 75 came from Yathrib to Mecca again during the pilgrimage season, 72 men and two or three women representing both Aws and Khazraj came and the *second pledge of Aqaba* was made. Soon after that, Muhammad ordered his companions to immigrate to Medina as discreetly as possible.

For the Aws and the Khazraj the immigration of Muhammad to Medina was a momentous thing, as that would enable them to counter the Jewish religious supremacy, as well as challenge the Quraish, their commercial rivals.

In other words the goals of Muhammad and that of Aws and Khazraj were met in this new pact between them. This pledge was not a pledge to proclaim and preach a religious message but it was a political/military alliance as the Sira points out by spelling out the exact words of the pact, Muhammad pledging to fight the "black and the red" of the people in his famous cry "blood , blood, destruction, destruction, I am of you and you

---

[63] http://www.al-eman.com/Islamlib/viewchp.asp?BID=251&CID=42#s4

are of me, I will war with those who you war with and will make peace those that you make peace with", i.e. the alliance lines were clear: Muhammad would lead the Aws and Khazraj, together with his Meccan Muslim followers to form an alliance that would defeat both the Jews (the red) and Pagan Meccans (the black), at a time when the Jews had thought that Muhammad had no bad intentions against them.

Details of the Second Pledge of Aqaba, known as the Pledge of War

On the night of this pledge, very secretly and discreetly Muhammad left Mecca with his uncle Abbas bin Abdel Muttalib to negotiate the terms of the pledge. Abbas knew that this alliance was an alliance of War. When they—the Aws and the Khazraj—had all gathered to pledge loyalty to Muhammad, Abbas spoke first. He asked them if they knew what they were supporting or what they were pledging their loyalty for.

They responded by saying that they knew what they were supporting. Abbas continued to inform the men that they were pledging their loyalty to fight the red (Jews) and the black (the unbelievers of Mecca, i.e. Quraish and all the other Meccan tribes). The men were told, "*So if you think that you have risked your wealth and your elders to be killed unnecessarily then hand him over. If you do so, then by Allah this would be shameful forever. But if you see that you are amenable to making this pledge of war with loyalty to Allah, sharing wealth, killing the so called nobles then you are the best of this world and hereafter.*"

After Abbas made them aware of what they were just about to do, Muhammad then spoke and said that by accepting their fealty, he was "***to prohibit himself from doing what they would forbid their wives and their children from doing.***" In essence they made a secret agreement to accept Muhammad as their political leader. Therefore, one sees that he had concluded a separate and secret pact that would ultimately seal the fate of the Jews prior to entering into an agreement with the Jews of Yathrib/Medina called later on the "Medina Pact." As we shall see, he would accuse the Jews of breaking the Medina Pact although he had already broken it himself long before it was agreed to.

So one of the delegates, Al Barra'[64], took Muhammad's hand in his own and said:

"By the one, who has sent you as a prophet, we will forbid you what we forbid our own, we pledge allegiance to you O apostle of Allah but we are the children of war, and the family of a warring clan, we have inherited this from generation after generation".

At this point Abu Haitham interjected saying:

"O apostle of Allah, between us and the Jews are ropes (meaning ties or links) and we are about to cut those and if we do that, then we might have disobeyed being in breach of our own agreement with them and so Allah may show you to come back to your people?"

This was very clever of him, as he stated clearly that they were about to *"cut the ropes"* - meaning the relationship - that they had with the Jews. They all probably knew that the so called new revelations in favour of the Jews were just a gimmick or a decoy, but wanted to be absolutely certain. Abu Haitham was saying that what if their enmity with the Jews at some point might be considered inappropriate, and then the messenger of Allah might change his mind and return back to Mecca! If that were to be the case, then the Aws and the Khazraj would be incurring a double loss for they would have lost the relationship with the Jews as well as that with Quraish having given Muhammad a refuge in their town.

According to the Sira, Muhammad smiled and said, ***"Blood, blood, destruction, destruction."*** This meant a declaration of war and killing and destruction. In other words, Muhammad was effectively saying: Behold I have settled the fate of the Jews. They are going to be annihilated and so will I get rid of Quraish as well. The old order will be fully done away with and I will establish a new order.

Listen to what Muhammad said next:

"I am of you and you are of me, I will fight (war) with those that you are (fighting) in war with, and I will make peace with those you will make peace with. See I am of you and you are of me, your enemies are

---

[64] http://www.al-eman.com/Islamlib/viewchp.asp?BID=249&CID=30 and http://sirah.al-islam.com/Display.asp?f=msr10064

mine and I will fight them, and those whom you make peace with I will make peace."

The die is cast

It is clear from the wording of the second 'Pledge of Aqaba' that the decision was taken to fight the Quraish and the Jews with the aim of either total conversion, submission, or elimination.

This is the authoritative version of the pledge in the recognized records of Islamic history.

It is clear from the wording of the pledge that it was a prior agreement and a desired intention to fight the Quraish (referred to as the black of the people) and of the Jews (as the red of the people), hence in effect, Muhammad had sealed the fate of the Jews of Medina or Yathrib well before reaching Yathrib.

It is noteworthy to mention that Muhammad was hoping that the Jews would embrace him and his new religion. However his undercover Pledge with the Arab tribes provided him with a failsafe, should those hopes not be realized. Anyway, he needed to buy some time to consolidate his new community, since at the time the Muslims were only a tiny minority in comparison to the Jews, and thus would not have been able to engage them head on. After all, the total number of immigrant Muslims known as Al Muhajirun were only a few hundred, while the Ansar or those in Yathrib who had embraced/ accepted Islam were in tens rather than in the hundreds. Concurrently, Muhammad had resorted to a diversion tactic by drawing up a separate pact with the Jews once he entered the city. So it too was self protecting. In other words the peace pact between the Muslims and the Jews was made or entered into, only due to the weakness of the Muslims in number and their capabilities.

Notice how Mohammed asked the Aws and the Khazraj to end their alliance with the Jews but at the same time he drew a peace pact with them himself, once he entered the city—though he had already settled and sealed their fate in the second pledge of Aqaba.

The Pact with the Jews of Medina

The "honeymoon" period with the Jews of Yathrib/Medina

On entering Medina he prayed towards their direction of prayer, namely Jerusalem, adopted the Jewish fast, and agreed to peaceful coexistence at a point in time when he had already sealed their fate.

No sooner had he entered Yathrib, than he drew up the "Medina Pact," that came to be known variously as a "Fraternal Pact,[65]" or the "Medina Constitution,[66]" sometimes known also as a friendship towards the Jews in which he declared religious tolerance, and freedom of belief, replacing unity of religion for ethnic solidarity.

All based on Sura 2:62, "***Verily! Those who believe and those who are Jews and Christians, and Sabians, whoever believes in Allah and the Last Day and do righteous good deeds shall have their reward with their Lord, on them shall be no fear, nor shall they grieve.***"

The most important stipulations of the pact were:

1. For the Jews was their religion and for the Muslims theirs…

2. The Jews had their patrons and persons, so did the Arabs…

3. The signatories or parties of this pact both Muslims and Jews had agreed to fight those that would attack either of them, and defend if their city was attacked and avert any danger…

4. There would be peace and cooperation between them…

5. Yathrib was a place of justice, and peace…

In other words Muhammad was walking cautiously because of his political and military weakness, as he increasingly realized that the Jews were most unlikely to turn in their masses and embrace Islam. This was one of the biggest blows to him. So it seems he decided to play it safe until he gathered sufficient strength to oust them.

---

[65] This is the text of the pact: http://sirah.alislam.com/Display.asp?f=rwd2146 http://sirah.al-islam.com/Display.asp?f=rwd2146 (please see Appendix M for full text of the pact)

[66] See http://www.qurtuba.edu.pk/thedialogue/The%20Dialogue/1_1/04--Islamic%20 Civilisatino.pdf

Ibn Taymiyyah states that in the beginning, the prophet was only commanded to strive or declare Jihad against the unbelievers with his tongue and not with his hand, and he was ordered to restrain from fighting them due to his inability and the inability of the Muslims. This was only until he immigrated to Medina and was now enabled by his new followers, that permission was granted for him by Allah to wage Jihad.[67]

While Ibn Kathir says in the early stage of Islam the believers in Mecca were commanded to forgive and be tolerant towards the unbelievers and be patient for the time being, they were already agitating and wishing for the command to fight or wage war, but their conditions would not

> **The Honeymoon Period for Jews and Islam, 622-624 AD**
>
> Muhammad's attempt to win over the Jews during the early days in Yathrib/Medina gave the illusion of peace, while preparing for war— and thus was the formative time for the development of Islamic policies toward the Jews...severe policies of condemnation and destruction which have no expiration date.

have allowed them to do so for number of reasons—for the smallness of their numbers, while their enemies were numerous, for this reason Jihad was not commanded until they were in Medina where they had a secure base and back up support.[68]

With such religious zeal among the early Muslim community, Medina became a formidable tower and a strong base for Muhammad to develop the political, military and legal components of the Islamic state, i.e. the Khaliphate. Within a short time the divine ordinance from Allah granting permission for Jihad was proclaimed.

Following the settlement of the Meccan Muslims and Mohammed in Medina the first phase of "tamkeen",[69] i.e. the consolidation and empowerment of the Muslims community, began, as their numbers increased and as preparations were undertaken to fight the "black of the people" meaning the Quraish. Muhammad now started to send secret skirmishing expedition

---

[67] الجواب الصحيح لم بد دين المسيح لابن تيمية 58/2. راجع: زاد المعاد 74/1 لابن القيم

[68] تفسير القُرآن العظيم لابن كثير 526/1

[69] See *Al Hijra: The Islamic Doctrine of Immigration* by Sam Solomon and Al Maqdisi

missions, hampering the flow of the Quraish's commercial caravans and its movements thus undermining the stability of Mecca.

Right from the start in Medina, physical Jihad was being portrayed as a major duty as per Sura 22:39, *"Permission to fight is given to those, who are fighting them, because they have been wronged, and surely, Allah is Able to give them victory,"* and, Sura 2:190,

> **The Advent of "History as Policy"**
>
> Starting in the so-called, "honeymoon period," Muhammad's treatment of the Jews was established as "precedent", with Muhammad's actions becoming Sunnah and thus, eternal law. Therefore, the treatment of the three Jewish tribes in Yathrib/Medina bear witness to the development of the enmity policies which would provide the framework for the Islamic Doctrine of Enmity.

"And fight in the Way of Allah those who fight you, but transgress not the limits. Truly, Allah likes not the transgressors."

Next, it was commanded to fight all the unbelievers everywhere, as in Sura 9:36, "...and fight against the Mushrikûn (polytheists, pagans, idolaters, disbelievers in the Oneness of Allâh) collectively, as they fight against you collectively..."

Having laid this foundational understanding of the background development in the early days in Medina, we can now bring into focus the central issue of who started the enmity.

The "honeymoon" is short-lived

The biographers of the Sira[70] state that as the Jews and in particular Banu Kaynuka were the first to breach the peace pact, they were the ones who broke their agreement with the Prophet and not the other way around. However if one examines what is reported by the Sira one would discover that it was Muhammad who breached his own peace pact with the Jews first, without any provocation on the part of the Jews.

The battle of Badr or rather the Badr invasion (624 AD) exposed the nature of Muhammad's mission in his methods when he concluded the

---

[70] http://sirah.al-islam.com/display.asp?f=hes2044.htm

victory by killing the notable leaders of the Quraish, confiscating their wealth, and taking their arms as booty. Following his brutal victory over the Quraish, now Muhammad turned his attention towards the Jews who had welcomed him when he arrived dejected and rejected by the Meccans.

Dealing with the Jewish Tribe of Banu Kaynuka

Shortly after the Battle of Badr, one day without any warning Muhammad went to their market place and addressed the leaders of Banu Kaynuka, warning them that either they embrace Islam or face death as did the Quraish in this recent battle. His words to them were, *"Take heed from Allah as he avenged himself of the Quraish, for you know I am a prophet sent by Allah as recorded in your scriptures."*[71]

This reference "as recorded in your scriptures" is key because Muhammad's charge against them was that they were in essence committing a sin worse than treason by having known that he was predicted to be the "expected one" but have refused to believe it and had removed these references from their scriptures. This is a type of "assumed enmity" as explained earlier.

It is reported by a famous Islamic scholar, Al Wakadi[72] that it was at this time that Allah revealed Sura 8:58, *"If you (Muhammad) fear treachery from any people throw back (their covenant) to them (so as to be) on equal terms (that there will be no more covenant between you and them). Certainly Allah likes not the treacherous."*

It is noteworthy to mention that the Jews had

Fate of the Banu-Kaynuka: Exile

They were the first of the tribes of the Jewish city of Yathrib/Medina to be faced with the Islamic ultimatum: Convert or face the sword! Being merchants, they had inhabited the inner city. After a 15 day siege, Muhammad pronounced the death sentence, but relented— allowing them to go into exile, each carrying whatever he could on one mule or horse. This first precedent was important to the evolving Islamic policy toward the Jews (and later Christians).

---

[71] http://www.al-eman.com/Islamlib/viewchp.asp?BID=249&CID=59

[72] كتاب المغازي الواقدي (1/180) :

not assisted the Quraish in any form or shape in the Battle of Badr. However it is clear that Muhammad was in breach of the first article of the pact in which it stated: "…to the Jews their religion and for the Muslims their religion…" So the questions that must be asked are: Why was he now demanding them in particular to convert to Islam or face death? What was the transforming factor? Why the Banu Kaynuka?

Muhammad chose to confront Banu Kaynuka first, as they were the smallest group of the three Jewish tribes in Medina, as well as being the most wealthy, with hardly any friends—as their relationship was in tatters with the rest of the Jewish community. Knowing this Muhammad picked upon them first as he knew well that no help will come from any direction.

One must recall that when he made the Medina Pact, he and his Muslim community were weak, and equally importantly, he had already concluded a covert treaty (the Pledge of Aqaba) which had nullified it in advance—laying the groundwork for the right moment to assert his control over the Jews (either by conversion or otherwise) Now after the victory of Badr, the size and numbers and strength of the Muslims had increased, so that they were now able to effectively mount a credible challenge according to their pre-determined purposes.

Predictably, Banu Kaynuka refused to convert to Islam, so the Muslims invented an unsupportable incident of a Jew insulting a Muslim woman as reported by Ibn Hisham[73]. It is reported by Ibn Hisham that Abdallah bin Ja'afar bin Al Masu'ar bin Mukharama from Abi Owan said that an Arab woman came to the market of Banu Kaynuka as they were goldsmiths, and while making her purchase they asked her to uncover her face but she refused. So the Jewish traders are said to have tied the back of her garment in a knot when she was unaware in a way that when she got up, the whole of her outer garment came off and she was exposed. So they–the Jewish traders—are reported to have burst out in laughter, so that one of the Arab Muslim men standing by attacked the Jewish trader and killed him.

---

[73] http://sirah.al-islam.com/display.asp?f=hes2045.htm

The story concludes that the Jews retaliated and killed the Muslim who had killed the Jewish trader. Hence there was anger amongst the Muslims against the Jews and there developed an animosity between them. Basically, this is the Islamic account of the first instance of admitted "enmity" between the Muslims and Jews.

Although the story claims that the Arab woman came into the Jewish marketplace fully covered, how can that be if this incident is reported to have taken place in year 3 of Hijra, while the veil was not legislated until year 5, and according to some other scholars as late as year 8?

Secondly how can a personal matter lead to the cancelation of a whole pact which was made with a community? Especially that the Medina pact stipulated that whoever wrongs as an individual will only be punished as an individual, and not the whole community collectively!

Clearly Muhammad's obvious and disgraceful breach of the pact forced the Muslim historians to invent this false story of an Arab woman and a Jewish goldsmith to justify Muhammad's revoking of the Medina Pact.

As Dr. Said Qemeni, a contemporary Egyptian Islamic scholar points out in his book,[74] "…all the irregularities in this story, that a Muslim who witnessed this whole incident drew his sword and killed the Jewish shopkeeper amazingly as Dr. Qemeni points out, the most important incident in the history of the first Islamic state does not record her name, her family or tribe, we don't know for sure if she was a Muslim. Not only that no one knows the name of the Arab Jewish gold smith who allegedly assaulted this woman, even worse there is no mention of any details of the Arab defender who attacked the shopkeeper, neither his name nor any of his personal or family details, nor did any of the Arab tribes seem to claim this deceased defender as their own." So it seems obvious, even coming from a renowned Islamic source, that this is nothing more than a made up story to defend the breach of the pact by Muhammad.

من كتاب الإسلاميات – قراءة اجتماعية سياسية للسيرة النبوية للمفكر المصري سيد القمني [74]

Interestingly Muhammad Rida[75] one of the leading scholars of Islam disputes this story too, nor it is mentioned by Muhammad's famous biographer, Ibn Ishaq or the most renowned Qur'anic expositors, Tabari, or the Islamic scholar, Ibn Sa'ad in his famous work, Tabakat.

Even though the Jews did not break or were in any breach of the Medina Pact this did not mean that Muhammad was going to remain faithful to it, as evidenced by his concurrent but covert "Pledge of Aqaba" with the Yathrib Arab tribes—for according to Qur'anic revelations, "allegiance" to non-Muslims is not valid as it contravenes a Muslim's faith. As Islam regards a non believer/Kaffer to be an enemy of Allah until he believes in Muhammad and embraces Islam as explained in the earlier section on the doctrine of Al-Walaa' wa Al-Baraa' (Allegiance and Rejection).

Muhammad surrounded Banu Kaynuka and put a siege around them for 15 days ending with their surrender. The siege had created a lot of fear in the hearts of the rest of the Jewish tribes as well, and it became clear that Mohammed was determined to kill them all at the same time—however the intervention of Abdallah ibn Salul one of the leading elders of Medina saved the day according to the Sira of ibn Hisham[76]. Ibn Salul was one of the chiefs of Khazraj. It was only his intervention that held Muhammad back, and allowed the Banu Kaynuka to leave the town, allowing them to take whatever their beast could take rather than be massacred on the spot. Of course they had to have a beast already, as they were forbidden to purchase any if they didn't have one.

Therefore one sees that from the battle of Badr onwards, Mohammed increased his strength and brutality even more, undertaking several operations of liquidating and assassinating all potential enemies, individually or collectively, among those who might be of any threat even on mere suspicion of causing a danger to his progress. To name few of many of

---

[75] : ص 182 محمد صلعم لمحمد رضا
[76] http://sirah.al-islam.com/Display.asp?f=rwd34, http://al-eman.com/Islamlib/viewchp.asp?BID=265&CID=1#s11, http://www.aleman.com/islamlib/viewchp.asp?BID=249&CID=60

those individuals he had murdered were: Abu Ifk, Asma bint Marwan[77], Ka'ab bin al Al Ashraaf[78], Abi Ra'af bin Abi Al Hakik and number of most respected leaders of Jewish tribes.

Ibn Al Hakik was a Jewish merchant from Khayber, who was assassinated by Abdallah bin A'tik at night while he lay asleep in his own house at the orders of Muhammad, as reported by Bukhari Hadith no 4038 and Fatheh al bari 7/345, Al Mughani wa Al Sharah al kabir vol 10/503.

Among the individuals who were seen to be in opposition to Muhammad was the Banu Nadir poet Ka'ab, who was assassinated for having composed a poem criticizing Muhammad. This had a devastating impact on the Jewish community, almost completely demoralising them and striking them with profound fear. Muhammad seeing and sensing that fear, ordered his followers to kill any Jew wherever they were to find them. It wasn't any ordinary killing that he ordered, but that the Jews were to be butchered, and their decapitated bodies to be thrown back in Jewish quarters to cast terror into hearts of the Jewish communities.

---

[77] From Ibn Sa`d's *Kitab al-Tabaqat al-Kabir*, translated by S. Moinul Haq, volume 2, pages 30-31.
SARIYYAH OF `UMAYR IBN `ADI : "Then (occurred) the sariyyah of `Umayr ibn `Adi Ibn Kharashah al-Khatmi against `Asma' Bint Marwan, of Banu Umayyah Ibn Zayd, when five nights had remained from the month of Ramadan, in the beginning of the nineteenth month from the hijrah of the apostle of Allah. `Asma' was the wife of Yazid Ibn Zayd Ibn Hisn al-Khatmi. She used to revile Islam, offend the prophet and instigate the (people) against him. She composed verses. Umayr Ibn Adi came to her in the night and entered her house. Her children were sleeping around her. There was one whom she was suckling. He searched her with his hand because he was blind, and separated the child from her. He thrust his sword in her chest till it pierced up to her back. Then he offered the morning prayers with the prophet at al-Medina. The apostle of Allah said to him: "Have you slain the daughter of Marwan?" He said: "Yes. Is there something more for me to do?" He [Muhammad] said: "No. Two goats will butt together about her. This was the word that was first heard from the apostle of Allah. The apostle of Allah called him `Umayr, "basir" (the seeing)."
http://www.answering-islam.org/Muhammad/Enemies/asma.html

[78] http://www.flex.com/~jai/satyamevajayate/mohwar2.html

Dealing with the Jewish Tribe of Banu Nadir

Just as Muhammad had cooked up charges against Banu Kaynuka, now he turned his attention to the tribe of Banu Nadir. According to Ibn Ishaq, Muhammad said that Allah had revealed to him that they were plotting to kill him by dropping a rock from a roof of a house on his head.

The actual underlying reason was that they were showing everyone from their scriptures that the central part of Muhammad's claims to prophethood and that he was the successor of all the previous prophets were false and they had the scriptures to prove it, so no wonder they had to be removed.

Muhammad laid a siege to the entire community forcefully evicting them, with whatever every three adults could manage to pack on the back of a camel, horse or donkey of their possession—that is "if" they had one of these, as no one was allowed to go out and purchase an animal if they didn't own one already.[79]

> ### The Fate of the Banu-Nadir: Exile
>
> They were the second tribe of the Jewish city of Yathrib/Medina to face the Islamic ultimatum. They were also besieged and forced into exile, this time ostensibly because of an alleged plot to kill Muhammad. Being primarily engaged in agriculture in addition to trading and money lending, they had lived outside the city in substantial fortresses—so that they were not as vulnerable militarily as their city-dwelling predessors. They, like the Banu Kaynuka before them, when forced into exile fled mostly to Khaybar where they would yet face another Islamic ultimatum.

Dealing with the Jewish Tribe of Banu Qurayza

Banu Qurayza was the third and the last Jewish tribe to remain. Like Banu Kaynuka and Banu Nadir before them, Banu Qurayza were a peaceful community of farmers and tradesmen. When Muhammad and his men laid siege to them after the Battle of the Ditch (626-627 A.D.)[80], Banu

---

[79] Reference to the exile and confiscation of Banu Nadir properties is given in Sura 59.

[80] Variation is dates based on different sources

Qurayza eventually surrendered with all they had (wealth and power) without a fight. However unlike Banu Kaynuka and Banu Nadir who had been granted exile, Muhammad ordered a wholesale slaughter of all males, boys as young as 14 years old, (any who had pubic hair) was slaughtered.[81]

At this event, over 800 men and boys were beheaded by Muhammad and his followers as per Sura 33:26, *"And those of the people of the Scripture who backed them (the disbelievers) Allâh brought them down from their forts and cast terror into their hearts, (so that) a group (of them) you killed, and a group (of them) you made captives,"* and Ibn Ishaq's account. Muhammad established this as a most certain Sunnah which would be most highly rewarded (by Allah on judgment day). As stated, Muhammad either personally or through consent killed, or rather butchered, more Jews than any others that he killed–be it pagan Arabs or otherwise.

> ### Fate of the Banu-Qurayza: Exile not granted!
>
> The last of the three tribes of the Jewish city of Yathrib/Medina—was not as fortunate as the others when faced with yet another unsubstantiated accusation of treachery—as when conquered, Muhammad chose not to grant them the option of exile, but instead brutally executed the male members of the tribe in front of their families, and enslaved the women and children. At this point in time, the "Dhimmi Laws" had not been introduced, as it would be following the invasion of Khaybar.

Muhammad not only beheaded innocent Jews of Banu Qurayza but even took a young and beautiful Jewess whose husband was beheaded in front of her own eyes for his sexual gratification.[82] The rest of the widows

---

[81] To separate adult men from the pre-pubescent boys, the youngsters were examined and if they had grown any pubic hair, it was enough to behead them **(Abu Dawud; see Ibn Ishaq, p. 466)**.
Sunan Abu-Dawud-Book 3=, No. 4390 Narrated Atiyyah al-Qurazi:
"I was among the captives of Banu Qurayzah. They (the Companions) examined us, and those who had begun to grow hair (pubes) were killed, and those who had not were not killed. I was among those who had not grown hair."

[82] The apostle had chosen one of their women for himself, Rayhana bint Amr . . . one of the women of . . . Qurayza, and she remained with him until she died, in his power. The apostle had proposed to marry and put a veil on her, but she said: "Nay, leave me in your power, for that will be easier for me and for you." So he left her. She had shown repugnance towards Islam when she was captured and clung to Judaism. (Ibn Ishaq, p. 466)

and surviving children he gave away as slaves to his men. The wealth accumulated by the Qurayza was also divided. Since the tribe had been a peaceful farming and trading community, according to Ibn Ishaq[83] there were not enough weapons and horses taken to suit Muhammad's tastes, so he obtained more of these by trading off some of the Qurayza women in a distant slave market.

Dealing with the Jews of Khaybar

Having dealt with Banu Kaynuka, Banu Nadir, and Banu Qurayza, the city of Medina was basically cleared of Jews and Muhammad set his mind to a campaign of eradicating all of the Jewish tribes in Arabia, but particularly from around Medina. In 628-629 A.D., he made a pre-emptive, sudden and unprovoked assault on the Jews of Khaybar. Khaybar was mostly a Jewish oasis town which was located approximately 100 miles from Medina in the North West part of Arabia.

Many of the exiled Banu Nadir from Medina in 625 A.D. had come to Khaybar to find refuge amongst this Jewish community.

Background and prelude to Khaybar

In 628 A.D., having broken the Jewish supremacy in Medina, Muhammad was ready to take on the Quraish so he marched to Mecca under the pretence of wanting to perform pilgrimage. However the Quraish sent a message requesting him to come the following year. After much negotiations, the Muslims entered a peace treaty with the Quraish, known as the Hudaibiya Treaty, ending the Muslim-Quraish wars. Some of his followers, however, were discontent at the terms Muhammad had agreed to—terms which he would later nullify and abrogate by conquering Mecca in less than 2 years.

Scholars agree that Muhammad's need to raise his prestige amongst his followers, which had been eroded by the Hudaibiya Treaty, was one reason for the unprovoked attack on Khaybar.

---

[83] Ibn Ishaq 693

The Khaybar oasis was divided into three regions: al-Natat, al-Shikk, and al-Katiba. Each of these regions had several fortresses, containing homes, storehouses and stables. Each fortress was occupied by a separate family and surrounded by cultivated fields and palm-groves.

Knowing the outcome of Muhammad's battles with the other Jewish tribes, the Jews of Khaybar put up fierce resistance, and the Muslims were forced to take the fortresses one by one. During the battle, the Muslims were able to prevent Khaybar's Arab allies (consisting of 4,000 men) from providing them with reinforcements. One reason given for this lack of support from their erstwhile allies, is that the Muslims were able to neutralize the pagan Arab Bedouins by buying them off.

Some say only 19 Jews died, while others report as many as 90, but in either case, Muhammad's brutality remained the same in the sense that he took Safiyya bint Huyayy as his wife[84], though her father and husband

---

[84] **Book 9; number 99:** Anas said: Captives were gathered at Khaybar. Dihyah (a Jihadi fighter) came and said: "Apostle of Allah, give me a slave-girl from the captives." He said : Go and take a slave-girl. He took Safiyaah daughter of Huyayy. A man then came to the Prophet (may peace be upon him) and said: "You gave Safiyaah daughter of Huyayy, chief lady of Quraizah and al-Nadir to Dihyah?" This is according to the version of Ya'qub. Then the version goes: "She is worthy of you." He said: "Call him along with her." When the Prophet (may peace be upon him) looked at her, he said to him: "Take another slave-girl from the captives. The Prophet (May peace be upon him) then set her free and married her.

Tabari writes on same subject:
"After the Messenger of God conquered al-Qamus, the fortress of Ibn Abi al-Huqyaq, Safiyaah bt. Huyayy b. Akhtab was brought to him, and another woman with her. Bilal, who was the one who brought them, led them past some of the slain Jews. When the woman who was with Safiyaah saw them, she cried out, struck her face, and poured dust on her head. When the Messenger of God saw her, he said, 'Take this she-devil away from me!' she commanded that Safiyaah should be kept behind him and that the Messenger of God had chosen her for himself."

Also, Sahih Bukhari, Volume 5, Book 59, Number 5 — Narrated by Anas:
The Prophet offered the Fajr Prayer near Khaybar when it was still dark and then said, "Allahu-Akbar! Khaybar is destroyed, for whenever we approach a (hostile) nation (to fight), then evil will be the morning for those who have been warned." Then the inhabitants of Khaybar came out running on the roads. The Prophet had their warriors killed, their offspring and woman taken as captives. Safiyaah was amongst the captives, She first came in the share of Dahya Alkali but later on she belonged to the Prophet. The Prophet made her manumission as her 'Mahr.' Muhammad was sixty (60) when he married Safiyaah, a young girl of seventeen. She became his eighth wife.

were both beheaded on the same day and he went into her on the same day of their beheading.

To hide the lascivious character of Muhammad, Muslim biographers often mention that he married Safiyaah before he slept with her. But they forget to mention that Muhammad did not follow the rule of a waiting period (three monthly periods) to sleep with Safiyaah. He slept with her in the same day she was captured.

Implications of the Khaybar Invasion

This time Muhammad realized that he needed the expertise of the Jews to cultivate the land and attend to the oasis, for two simple reasons:

1. He needed his men to fight his wars and subjugate the rest of Arabia to Islam, and

2. He needed the Jews and their expertise to cultivate the land and manage the oasis for continued supply for himself and his troops.

After securing paragon beautiful Safiyaah daughter of Huyayy Muhammad has had sex with this young Safiyaah in the tent, on their way back to Medina on the same night. Muhammad asked Bilal, to fetch Safiyaah to his (Muhammad's) camp. Bila brought Safiyaah and her cousin straight across the battlefield strewn with dead and close by the corpses of Kinana and his cousin. The two cousin sisters of Safiyaah shrieked in terror when they witnessed the grotesque scene of the slain dead bodies of their dearest relatives that they had to cross over. They tremulously begged a stone-hearted Bilal for mercy but to no avail. When they were brought to Muhammad, he cursed the panic-stricken cousins as devilish and cast his mantle around Safiyaah indicating that she was to be his own. Muhammad consoled a frustrated Dhiya by giving him Safiyaah's cousin sisters. According to Ibn Sa'd Prophet Muhammad purchased Safiyaah from Dhiyah for seven camels. On the same night (during the day her husband and all relatives were slaughtered) that Muhammad took possession of Safiyaah, he hastened to his tent to sleep with her.

Here is what Ibn Sa'd writes:

Islamic intolerance:

Book 09, Number 4366: It has been narrated by 'Umar b. al-Khattib that he heard the Messenger of Allah (may peace be upon him) say: "I will expel the Jews and Christians from the Arabian Peninsula and will not leave any but Muslim."

Bukhari Volume 4, Book 5, Number 76 Narrated 'Abdullah bin 'Umar: Allah's Apostle said, "You (i.e. Muslims) will fight with the Jews till some of them will hide behind stones. The stones will (betray them) saying, 'O 'Abdullah (slave of Allah)! There is a Jew hiding behind me; so kill him.'"

So Muhammad discussed the terms of surrender of the Jews of Khaybar. Here are some of the stipulations of his treaty with them, known as the Khaybar Treaty which established for the first time what would be known as the "Dhimmi Laws" governing the "People of the Book":

1. He declared them to be Dhimmis, i.e. people of obligation, Muhammad's obligation to protect them. In exchange for certain terms, their lives were spared.

2. Their wealth and land passed over to Muhammad, and from then on they had to pay land tax known as Kharaj, as they were no longer landlords but tenants,

3. Every year they were required to pay half of their produce as "humiliation tax" called Jizya,[85] (The word Jizya, comes from the root word, jazz', which means either punishment or reward)

4. They were not to be regarded as equal to Muslims,

5. They were not preach their religion or attempt to convert any of the Muslims,

6. They had no right to bear arms as their protection was guaranteed by Muhammad.

The agreement with the Jews of Khaybar served as an important precedent for Islamic Law in determining the status of Dhimmis,[86] (non-Muslims under Muslim rule).

The victory in Khaybar greatly raised the status of Muhammad among his followers and local Bedouin tribes who, seeing his power, swore allegiance to Muhammad and converted to Islam. The captured

---

[85] **Sahih Muslim writes:Book 00, Number 3759:** Ibn Umar (Allah be pleased with them) reported: Allah's Messenger (may peace be upon him) handed over the land of Khaybar (on the condition) of the share of produce of fruits and harvest, and he also gave to his wives every year one hundred wasqs: eighty wasqs of dates and twenty wasqs of barley. When 'Umar became the caliph he distributed the (lands and trees) of Khaybar, and gave option to the wives of Allah's Apostle (may peace be upon him) to earmark for themselves the land and water or stick to the wasqs (that they got) every year. They differed in this matter. Some of them opted for land and water, and some of them opted for wasqs every year. 'A'isha and Hafsa were among those who opted for land and water.

[86] See Bat Ye'or The Dhimmies Jews and Christian under Islam

booty and weapons strengthened his army, and he captured Mecca just 18 months after Khaybar.

From the time of the massacre of the Banu Qurayza tribe, Muhammad declared and established the killing of any Jew anywhere as a definitive Sunnah, (in this sense an action approved of by Muhammad) both as vocalized and enacted Sunnah, by stating that,[87] "*...whoever amongst the Jewish men you meet, kill them.*"

Henceforth there have been many Hadiths regarding the killing of the Jews

---

The Khaybar Invasion Unveils a New Policy toward Jews (and Christians)

The so-called "Dhimmi Laws" implemented first at Khaybar established a fourth option of response to the Islamic ultimatum for conquered Jews and Christians—the other three being: Conversion, exile or death, which were the terms imposed earlier on the three tribes of Yathrib/Medina. THIS FOURTH OPTION IS A SEVERE AND INSECURE FORM OF "CONTAINMENT" which would allow the "People of the Book" an arbitrary status within Islam, wherein they could keep their faith under severe legal restrictions, while remaining subject to the whims of the Muslim authorities of the day, who could refuse to grant this status, or once granted, either modify or revoke it outright.

---

including the famous one that "*Even the trees and the stones will cry out saying: O Muslim slave of Allah there is a Jew hiding behind me come and kill him,*" and "*...only when the whole earth has been purged of the Jewish race then and only then the end will come...*"

It is clear from the foregoing that it was Muhammad who instituted the enmity from the beginning of his mission in Mecca, who brought it to fruition in Medina, who breached the peace pact, who continued to attack Jewish communities unprovoked throughout Arabia—claiming that it had been revealed to him that Allah and his apostle were dissolving their treaties and pacts with the non-Muslims, not the other way around. Sura 9:1, "*Freedom from (all) obligations (is declared) from Allâh and His Messenger (SAW) to those of the Mushrikûn (polytheists, pagans, idolaters, disbelievers in the Oneness of Allâh), with whom you made a treaty.*"

---

[87] من ظفرتم به من رجال يهود فاقتلوه

Of course, all the atrocities that Muhammad committed based on the above revelations are regarded as a proper "Sunnah" to be emulated by all Muslims—hence limitless hate and enmity without exception towards the Jews everywhere at all times.

History as Policy: Why learn about 7th century battles?

As you read these exotic names—Bani Kaynuka, Banu Nadir, etc—one may have the tendency to skip ahead, thinking "What does this have to do with today?" Or, "But we are in the 21st century now, things are different!" Little do you know that Muhammad prepared the mechanism within his actions in Mecca, Medina, and Arabia in executing these battles and originating the related policies and doctrines—which are all "Sunnah" and hence part and parcel of the Islamic jurisprudence regarding the treatment of Jews, as well as Christians, and the "Other"—so that whatever happened in these battles could be replicated in the future. Meaning, these battles/historic incidents have influenced other situations and circumstances since that time, and continue to do so even as we speak.

We will give two examples below of cases wherein modern situations have been dealt with according to the historic patterns incorporated into the Qur'an and other Islamic source books.

Yathrib/Medina Poet and Danish Cartoons of 2005

For example, we have discussed the situation earlier of the Yathrib/Medina poet "Ka'ab Ibn Al-Ashraf" of the Jewish tribe, Banu Nadir, who was aggrieved and outraged at the death of many of his friends among the notables of the Quraish in Mecca during the Battle of Badr (624 A.D), and in response wrote poems of lament for those Meccans who were killed.

Muhammad expressed his desire to get rid of Ka'ab asking those around him, "who will take care of him?" A plan was developed, whereby Ka'ab was betrayed by a close personal friend who, with Muhammad's "consent" and "blessings", undertook the action to "defend" the honour of Muhammad and Islam by pretending to agree with Ka'ab about his criticisms of Muhammad, only to get him alone and murder him in a brutally humiliating way.

Thus, based on this, and several other historic incidents, Muhammad established the initial principle both by claiming Qur'anic injunctions[88] as well as establishing it as Sunnah which later become enforceable for all generations through Shariah Law—that to ridicule or insult his person in any way, or to be critical in regard to what he said, did, or consented to—is to insult Allah and Islam—thus making oneself an "enemy" of Allah with prescribed criminal penalties including death as explained by Ibn Taymiyya[89] and Kadi Ayyad[90] earlier.

The most recent contemporary application of this Islamic principle is the well-known worldwide furore among Muslims in response to the series of twelve editorial cartoons containing depictions of Muhammad which were published in the Danish newspaper Jyllands-Posten on September 30, 2005. The responsible Danish cartoonist Kurt Westergaard has been placed under governmental security protection, but despite that there was an attempt on his and his family's life as recently as January 4, 2010[91].

This principle, illustrated by the Poet Ka'ab incident, is only one of many instances within the Islamic jurisprudence which backs up the principle that Muhammad is beyond any form of criticism, and that to portray his character negatively is a serious or a grave crime.

Hudaybiah Treaty compared to the Oslo Agreements

The Hudaybiah Treaty which Muhammad signed in 628 A.D. with the Meccan pagans had displeased some of his closest companions, including Omar Ibn Al-Khattab, who later became the 2nd Khalifah after Muhammad's death. At that time, Omar is reported to have stated that Muhammad had made too many concessions to the Meccans. Although Hudaybiah was supposed to have been a 10 year treaty to be renewed, Muhammad abrogated it in less than two years, after a local incident of a dispute between two Meccans, in which one of the contenders died. Muhammad

---

[88] Sura 33:53 "…it isn't right for you to vex the prophet of Allah…", Also Suras 59:4, and 8:12-13.

[89] See footnote no's. 47a & b

[90] See footnote no. 52

[91] http://www.guardian.co.uk/world/2010/jan/04/danish-cartoonist-axe-attack

seized upon this incident, claiming that the deceased was a Muslim and was killed because he was a Muslim, thus concluding that the Meccans had violated the terms. This arbitrary decision led to the abrogation of the treaty and the occupation of Mecca by the Muslims.

Some current Muslim apologists insist that Muhammad did not break the treaty, but that he reacted in response to a (highly disputed) incident whereby some 20 Muslims were killed by the Meccans, thus violating their part of the treaty. However, even if this were true, it would not constitute grounds to retaliate by conquering Mecca and imposing Islam on the whole population—which is exactly what was reflected in Sura 110 (Called the Conquest Sura), "*1 When comes the Help of Allâh (to you, O Muhammad (Peace be upon him) against your enemies) and the conquest (of Makkah), 2 And you see that the people enter Allâh's religion (Islâm) in crowds, 3 So glorify the Praises of your Lord, and ask for His Forgiveness. Verily, He is the One Who accepts the repentance and forgives.*" [Al-Hilali]

Just like the foregoing, shortly after Yasser Arafat signed the 1994 Oslo Agreements, hoped by everybody to be the "final settlement" of the Israeli-Palestinian conflict, he gave more than one speech in which he stated that Oslo is similar to Hudaybiah. This simply means that it was expedient to sign up now to be able to conquer thereafter at the first given opportunity.

Knowing the above selective examples of historic incidents during Muhammad's establishment of the Muslim Ummah in Medina, and the Islamic Caliphate in Arabia—examples which were incorporated into the Qur'an and ultimately into the body of Shariah law which now governs or influences Muslim countries and societies—one can see clearly that these incidents were not just a "one off" but are historic with an enforceable validity, thus in fact are a part of our present and future.

As we approach the next chapter on Jerusalem, one will see how much so, and more importantly, why the entire battle for truth against the claims of Islam must rage first toward Israel, before coming in full force against the entire free world—so that Israel, as well as Jerusalem, is indeed in the "Eye of the Storm", taking the pressure meant eventually for us all.

chapter 6
Jerusalem:
The Eye of the Storm

Why Jerusalem?!

Claims and counterclaims

Now we turn to consider Jerusalem. Readers around the world should be fully familiar with the constant announcements by Palestinian, Arab and non-Arab Muslim leaders and proponents that in any political settlement of the conflict, Jerusalem is to become the purely Muslim/Arab capital of the Palestinian state to be. Of course, there is the opposite counterclaim by Israel that Jerusalem is to be the capital of Israel, and today, it is[92]. The historical record on the legitimacy of the Israeli claim is clear and fully supported by massive amounts of evidence. But what is the basis for the Muslim/Arab claim?

> **Muhammad's "Night Journey" Claims:**
>
> The Night Journey…a dream or vision by Muhammad (full original text below) in 621 A.D. bears the only witness to the Islamic claim to Jerusalem and the Holy Land…while at one fell swoop legitimizing the land and substantiating Muhammad's own claims to be the Seal of the Prophets by giving account of having received the imprimatur for this mission in person from Abraham, Moses, Jesus, and the other prophets…and afterwards leading them in prayer…before finally meeting with Allah himself in the seventh heaven.

---

[92] Although Jerusalem is Israel's capital housing all the branches of government, the international community has not agreed to recognize Israel's decision, pending a political settlement on the issue. This demonstrates the immense political power of the Muslim states in keeping the pressure on all countries on this issue. Hence all foreign embassies are located in Tel Aviv, and not Jerusalem.

How and why is Jerusalem regarded as an Islamic sanctity?

Since Muhammad lived and died in what is presently known as Saudi Arabia, never having ventured outside—at least not in terms of any conquering expedition—how then could there be grounds for an Islamic claim to Jerusalem? Furthermore, after his death, Muslims invaded all the surrounding countries but none of them were declared as a sacred territory, so why Jerusalem?

Muhammad's vision establishes Islamic claim to Jerusalem

To understand how Jerusalem has been incorporated or grafted into the Islamic belief system, one has to understand the interactions between the doctrine of "Al-Isra' wal Mi'raaj" and the Islamic doctrine of Fitrah[93]. The "Isra' wal Mi'raaj" is a two-part visionary journey with the first leg being from Mecca to Jerusalem with a brief layover, and the second leg, from Jerusalem upwards to all the 7 heavens and beyond to meet Allah himself, descending back the same way through Jerusalem to Mecca—all carried out in one night.

The Al-Isra' is recorded in Sura 17:1, *"Glorified be He above all that (evil) they associate with Him Who took His slave for a journey by night from Al-Masjid-al-Haram (at Mecca) to the farthest mosque (in Jerusalem), the neighbourhood whereof We have blessed, in order that We might show him of Our (proofs, evidences, lessons, signs, etc.). Verily, He is the All-Hearer, the All-Seer."*

> **Muhammad's report of his visionary ride on the steed "Al-Burak" to Jerusalem**
> *(Excerpts from Sira account)*
>
> "Al-Burak was brought to me, and it was a white animal bigger than a donkey and smaller than a mule. One stride of this creature covered a distance as far as it could see. I rode on it and it took me to Bayt Al-Maqdis (Jerusalem), where I tethered it at the hitching post of the Prophets..." *[Excerpt #1]*
>
> "Al-Burak was brought to the Prophet on the Night of the Isra' with his saddle and reins ready for riding. The animal shied, and Jibril said to him: 'Why are you doing this? By Allah, no one has ever ridden you who is more honoured by Allah than him.' At this, Al-Burak started to sweat." *[Excerpt #2]*

---

[93] See Chapter 4 on the Fitrah.

The story goes, with diverse variations, that one night as Muhammad was sleeping in the neighbourhood of the Ka'aba in Mecca he was awakened by angel Gabriel who escorted him to a winged steed called Al-Burak, and with Muhammad mounted, they journeyed together from Mecca to Jerusalem. On the way there they encountered several good as well as evil powers, making brief stops at Hebron and Bethlehem.

Muhammad leads the prophets in Islamic prayer in Jerusalem

At Jerusalem they (Gabriel and Muhammad) met Abraham, Moses, Jesus, and all other previous prophets. Islamic ritual prayer (Salat) was performed corporately, with Muhammad acting as Imam—thereby asserting his authority and taking precedence over all the other assembled prophets. This was not an Abrahamic Jewish form of prayer, or what Jesus taught in terms of prayer, but it was an Islamic form of prayer which Gabriel is said to have taught Muhammad. All the prophets, being Muslims, followed Muhammad's lead in an Islamic ritual prayer.

> ### Muhammad presides over the prophets in Jerusalem and/or in Paradise during Isra'
>
> [Some scholars say that to honor Muhammad, Allah sent all the prophets to Jerusalem for ritual communal prayer with Muhammad as their Imam. Others say he assembled them in Paradise. The following Hadith gives Muhammad's words regarding the significance of this event].
>
> **"I will be the leader of the sons of Adam on the Day of Resurrection and the first for whom the grave will be opened and the first to intercede and the first whose intercession will be accepted."**
>
> [Hadith Narrated by Al-Muslim, 2278. See Appendix H for details on supremacy of Muhammad during Night Journey]

The details of the visionary journey are not found in the Qur'an but it is extensively elaborated upon in the Sira and some in the Hadith.

Night Journey affirms Muhammad's supremacy

This is meant to show the supremacy of Muhammad over all the prophets and their subjugation to him personally and thereby confirming their recognition of his alleged calling as the Seal of the Prophets.[94] In a related Hadith, Muhammad expresses his self-realization of his supremacy over all mankind.[95]

Early scholars differed among themselves as to whether this was a bodily experience, or if it was just a vision, or if his spirit travelled while his body remained behind. (Page 553 E.J. Brill's First encyclopaedia of Islam 1913-1936).

Then there were others who have questioned the whole authenticity and validity of the same; for instance Gabriel was mentioned for the first time in Medina [96]Islamic ritual prayers were legislated and established in Medina[97], and so was the ritual of the ablution[98]. The order to pray for five times was received at the end of this trip when Muhammad encountered Allah himself (while being coached by Moses)[99] yet he seems to precede the events by leading the rest of the prophets and so on.

Gradually belief in Isra' or Muhammad's night journey, became an integral part of the Islamic main tenets and central to the Islamic doctrine—it is from this alleged vision/experience that the whole of Jerusalem was retroactively laid claim to for Islam, and thus became the furthest-most Mosque.

Muhammad "inherits" all previous prophets and revelations

The vision of Isra' wal Mi'raaj served well at the time and still serves as proving that Muhammad as the final prophet, is the Imam of all the Prophets, and therefore "he inherits all of them" as he is the custodian and

---

[94] More details on the supremacy of Muhammad are provided in Appendices D, E and F.

[95] Muhammad announces his supremacy with divine attributes as in Hadith 61.1.1: 4 Malik related to me from Ibn Shihab from Muhammad ibn Jubayr ibn Mutim that the Prophet, may Allah bless him and grant him peace, said, "I have five names. I am Muhammad. I am Ahmad. I am al-Mahi (the effacer), by whom Allah effaces kufr. I am al-Hashir (the gatherer), before whom people are gathered. I am al-Aqib (the last)." (Muwatta.1:3,4)

[96] See Sura 2:97-98

[97] As per the concensus of Islamic scholars

[98] Sura 5:6

[99] See section below on the Al Isra' wal Mi'raaj

reformer of their people.[100] He is the sole inheritor and only Muhammad can have the final word in their legacy as he is the only one appointed by Allah with the full consent of all the prophets, so that Muhammad is the disposer and executor of their affairs and valuables.

In plain words, he inherits "all of them" meaning that he is the custodian of their message and the people to

> ## Muhammad's Universal Mission and Inheritance
>
> This "inheritance" is visually portrayed in the Night Journey—in terms of the fellowship and fealty of all the previous prophets and the depiction of the "land," including Jerusalem, the Holy Land and the entire world, as being under his authority as the final prophet of Allah. In a later Hadith confirming the vision, Muhammad stated, *"The earth has been declared unto me a mosque..."*
>
> [Hadith #31901 Kanz Al-Umal]

whom they were sent, so that Jesus would say to him, *"I told my people, the Jews and my followers, that you are to come after me. It is your responsibility, Muhammad, to defend, intercede for them or punish them."* Moses would say likewise, so would Abraham, while Adam would say to him, *"All of my progeny has been covenanted by Allah to believe in him and to believe in you, Muhammad. For you are the most honoured and esteemed of all the prophets. You are the Imam of all of them. You are the master of all creation."* So this explains what the Sura above means when it says that Muhammad is the inheritor and custodian of the prophets. Any Islamic book opens with praise to Muhammad along these lines.[101]

As Islam is the "religion of Allah," all the prophets are Muslims, who were merely heralds of this greatest prophet, so the argument goes that it is only appropriate that their most sacred city must be declared Islamic and maintained as such.

So, based on Al-Isra' wa Al-Mi'raaj or Night Journey he has declared Jerusalem as an Islamic city, a sacred one in line with Mecca and Medina which was later conquered by his followers. (Some 70 years after the death

---

[100] See Appendix F for more details

[101] The two references in this paragraph are eschatological and all are contained in the same passage. See Appendix B for further eschatological details

of Muhammad, the Umayyad dynasty built both the Al-Aqsa Mosque and the Dome of the Rock).

The text from the Sira (Muhammad's biography) to follow is one of many reputedly verbatim accounts, reportedly by Muhammad himself, of his Night Journey vision. This and other related accounts are included and commented upon in the Sira and the Hadith, and were used as a basis for a wide ranging set of claims and doctrines as explained earlier. We have included the full text of one of these accounts here because as a narrative account it gives a complete and vivid picture of the entire vision in Muhammad's own words. However, one needs to examine the various appendices covering other accounts and related issues in order to be able to comprehend the full doctrinal scope and impact on Islam and one's understanding of it.

This is how the story is reported in the Islamic manuals:

Text of the Al-Isra' wa Al-Mi'raaj from Islamic manuals

Isra' wal Mi'raaj
(Vision of Muhammad's Night Journey)

It is narrated on the authority of Anas ibn Malik (r.a.) that the Messenger of Allah (peace and blessings be upon him) said: "Al-Burak was brought to me, and it was a white animal bigger than a donkey and smaller than a mule. One stride of this creature covered a distance as far as it could see. I rode on it and it took me to Bayt Al-Maqdis (Jerusalem), where I tethered it at the hitching post of the Prophets. Then I entered and prayed two Rak'ahs there, and came out. Jibril brought me a vessel of wine and a vessel of milk, and I chose the milk.

"Jibril said: You have chosen the Fitrah (natural instinct).' Then I was taken up to the first heaven and Jibril asked for it to be opened. It was said, 'Who are you?' He said, 'Jibril.' It was said, 'Who is with you?' He said, 'Muhammad.' It was asked, 'Has his

Mission started?' He said, 'His Mission has started.' So it was opened for us, and there I saw Adam, who welcomed me and prayed for good for me. Then I was taken up to the second heaven and Jibril asked for it to be opened. It was said, Who are you?' He said, 'Jibril.' It was said, Who is with you?' He said, 'Muhammad.' It was asked, 'Has his Mission started?' He said, 'His Mission has started.' So it was opened for us, and there I saw the two maternal cousins, Yahya and Isa, who welcomed me and prayed for good for me. Then I was taken up to the third heaven and Jibril asked for it to be opened. It was said, Who are you?' He said, 'Jibril.' It was said, Who is with you?' He said, 'Muhammad.' It was asked, 'Has his Mission started?' He said, 'His Mission has started.' So it was opened for us, and there I saw Yusuf, who had been given the beautiful half (half beauty of the world). He welcomed me and prayed for good for me. Then I was taken up to the fourth heaven and Jibril asked for it to be opened. It was said, Who are you?' He said, 'Jibril.' It was said, Who is with you?' He said, 'Muhammad.' It was asked, 'Has his Mission started?' He said, 'His Mission has started.' So it was opened for us, and there I saw Idris, who welcomed me and prayed for good for me. – then (the Prophet) said: Allah says: "And We raised him to a high station."

[Then he resumed his narrative]: "Then I was taken up to the fifth heaven and Jibril asked for it to be opened. It was said, Who are you?' He said, 'Jibril.' It was said, Who is with you?' He said, 'Muhammad.' It was asked, 'Has his Mission started' He said, 'His Mission has started.' So it was opened for us, and there I saw Harun, who welcomed me and prayed for good for me. Then I was taken up to the sixth heaven and Jibril asked for it to be opened. It was said, Who are you?'

He said, 'Jibril'. It was said, 'Who is with you?' He said, 'Muhammad.' It was asked, 'Has his Mission started?' He said, 'His Mission has started.' So it was opened for us, and there I saw Musa, who welcomed me and prayed for good for me. Then I was taken up to the seventh heaven and Jibril asked for it to be opened. It was said, 'Who are you?' He said, 'Jibril.' It was said, 'Who is with you?' He said, 'Muham—mad.' It was asked, 'Has his Mission started?' He said, 'His Mission has started.' So it was opened for us, and there I saw Ibrahim, who was leaning back against the Much—Frequented House (Al—Bayt Al—Ma'mur).

"Every day seventy thousand angels enter it, then they never come back to it again. Then I was taken to Sidrat Al—Muntaha (the Lote tree beyond which none may pass), and its leaves were like the leaves [ears] of elephants and its fruits were like jugs, and when it was veiled with whatever it was veiled with by the command of Allah, it changed, and none of the creatures of Allah can describe it because it is so beautiful. Then Allah revealed that which He revealed to me. He enjoined on me fifty prayers every day and night. I came down until I reached Musa, and he said, 'What did your Lord enjoin on your Ummah' I said, 'Fifty prayers everyday and night.' He said, 'Go back to your Lord and ask Him to reduce (the burden) for your Ummah, for your Ummah will not be able to do that. I tested the Children of Israel and found out how they were.' So I went back to my Lord and said, 'O Lord, reduce (the burden) for my Ummah for they will never be able to do that.' So He reduced it by five. I came back down until I met Musa and he asked me, 'What did you do?' I said, '(My Lord) reduced (my burden) by five.' He said, 'Go back to your Lord and ask Him to reduce (the burden) for your Ummah.' I kept going back between my Lord and Musa, and (my Lord) reduced it by five each time, until He said, 'O Muhammad, these are five prayers every day and night, and for every prayer there is (the reward of) ten, so they are (like) fifty prayers. Whoever wants to do some-thing good then does not do it, one good deed will be recorded for him, and if he does it, ten good deeds will be recorded for him. Whoever wants to do something evil and does not do it, no evil deed will be recorded for him, and if he does it, one evil deed will be recorded for him.'

"I came down until I reached Musa, and told him about this. He said: 'Go back to your Lord and ask him to reduce (the burden) for your Ummah, for they will never be able to do that.' I had kept going back to my Lord until I felt too shy."

This version was also recorded by Muslim. Imam Ahmad recorded Anas saying that Al-Burak was brought to the Prophet on the Night of the Isra' with his saddle and reins ready for riding. The animal shied, and Jibril said to him: "Why are you doing this By Allah, no one has ever ridden you who is more honored by Allah than him." At this, Al-Burak started to sweat.

Night Journey vision fails to impress the Jews

Muhammad had thought that his claims of being with the prophets and the Jewish Patriarchs would draw the Jews towards him, and convince them to turn and accept him as their Expected One—due to his claims of being close to Moses, that he was being counselled by Moses yet keeping himself superior as the final intercessor before Allah. However none of his claims made any difference to the Jews, but to the contrary he was ridiculed, and laughed at. And above all they directly challenged him in his claims—for they had the scriptures to prove their point, and this intensified his hate towards them. Therefore Muhammad set out to not only to oust them but to take over all that was and is Jewish or Jewish-owned in any form or shape.

Of particular importance to Muhammad was the physical ownership of what we know today as the historic Jewish "Holy Land" of Israel.[102] Muhammad was not satisfied by what he did in terms of expulsions from Medina, mass executions, and the imposition of humiliating laws (known as "Dhimmi Laws"). He wanted to own their most cherished land. This was accomplished by instituting several doctrines (e.g. utter supremacy of Muhammad, legislating the 5-times ritual prayer, exclusive intercessory rights of Muhammad), some directly based on the Isra' wal-Mi'raaj (night journey) as reflected in the Islamic Shariah regulations on "Waqf" (endowments).

Waqf: Islamic claim to the whole of Israel as Muslim Land[103]

Question: Do the Jews have a historical right to this land called 'Palestine'?

The claim by all so-called monotheistic religions, that is to say Judaism, Christianity, and Islam, over Jerusalem as their religious centre has made Jerusalem an international focal point, thus making it a doctrinal central crisis focal point as well.

Added to that, the exclusive claim by the Muslims of the city, based on the night visionary journey as an Islamic city—while fully nullifying the historical and religious rights of both the Jews and the Christians over Jerusalem multiplies the complexity of any resolution. In fact, Islamic claims are even more extensive than that. as Muslims regard all of Palestine / Israel proper, Gaza, and the West Bank as fully Islamic territory.

Muslims the world over believe that the whole of Israel and Jerusalem in particular is an Islamic land known as "Waqf."

---

[102] Called by the Romans and later the Muslim Arabs as, "Palestine."

[103] Further details from Islamic authoritative sources are provided in Appendices: B, C, F, G, H, I, J, K, and L. Also, note Appendix J, demonstrating that Muhammad appropriated Hebron as a Waqf to a particular clan, many years even before a single Muslim soldier reached Jerusalem.

Waqf is an Arabic word which means to stop, or to prevent. In Islamic legal terminology it means, to protect, to prevent a thing (land) from becoming the property of a third person. There are various kinds of Waqf and the four Jurisprudence schools of Sunni Islam have differed in their points of view. Please check the various fatwa listed in the Appendix (Appendices B, C, F, G, H, I, J, K, and L).

In the case of Islamic claims towards Jerusalem, Waqf means this land is the "endowment" by Allah, and thus the perpetual property of the Muslim Ummah, and as such, it is regarded as sacred as a whole.

This position was affirmed by "The Fourth Conference of the Academy of Islamic Research" entitled, "Arab Theologians on Jews and Israel" held at Al-Azhar University in the autumn of 1968. This conference "was convened…to discuss the fundamentals of the Middle East conflict, particularly its spiritual-theological significance and its historical antecedents.[104]" Therefore this conference constituted an affirmation by "fiat" of the official Islamic position on "Waqf." (Described in Chapter 3)

Islamic Waqf is not subject to negotiation

But in particular the specific Islamic sites, such as the Dome of the Rock and other designated sites, must be held to be beyond the bounds of non-Muslims. As such, no part or parcel of the Waqf is to be sold, traded with or subject to any negotiations, whatever the reason may be—and if lost for any reason, it must be fought for until it is regained no matter how long it takes, or what the cost. However the Muslim scholars have neither made it clear nor do they agree as to whether the whole of Palestine is Waqf or not, and if so, what about the Jewish and the Christian holy sites? What about the houses and the businesses that are there, particularly those that are owned by non-Muslims?

Do all these come under an Islamic Waqf? And if so, why did the Muslims of Palestine willingly sell their lands, houses and farms to the Jews in the 1930's?

---

[104] See Page 7 of: D. L. Green editor, "Arab Theologians on Jews and Israel", based "The Fourth Conference of the Academy of Islamic Resarch," held at the Al-Azhar University, Cairo, Egypt, Autumn of 1968.

Yet they are the ones who are belatedly declaring it to be Waqf. Didn't they know when they sold it, that the sale contract was null and void from the beginning—that is, from the Islamic point of view? This explains why the strange phenomenon whereby Jewish landowners in the 30's and 40's who paid for these properties are now being asked to give them back. An analogy would be if a citizen of any community or country were to try and sell communal property such as a bridge or a public building—like the infamous stories of people in England who cunningly "sold" the "London Bridge" to naïve purchasers. Therefore, it is clear that the Muslims were depending on the legal status of the land being a "Waqf", and took the money knowing that under Islam their "rights" could not be breached.

But why is only Palestine an Islamic Waqf when there are sacred Islamic sites all over the place outside of Palestine? How come these have not been declared as Islamic Waqf?

Nevertheless, Jerusalem itself has been officially declared to be an Islamic Waqf so that it must be solely under Muslim jurisdiction and there-fore no Muslim ruler should let go of it at any cost!

The Islamic proponents and the media have resorted to portraying Palestine as the land of the Palestinians stating that the Jews are occupiers and foreigners, thus diverting attention to the political and away from the religiously focused Islamic view, so that very few outside the Middle East are aware of these outrageous doctrinal claims to the land.

Clearly these religious claims that originated in the 7th century, based on nothing but an ambiguous dream /experience of one man, cannot trump the history of the Jewish people in this land. Whoever reads history will discover that the Jews have been on this land for 4000 years prior to any Muslim presence, which was unjustly and falsely called Palestine by the Roman Empire in their effort to discredit the Jews after the Bar Kochba revolt against Rome in A.D. 135. As the "final insult" to the Jews, the Emperor Hadrian renamed the Roman "Provincia Judaea" as the "Provin-cia Syria Palaestina," thus, not only changing its name but its identity further by combining it with Syria, its long-time adversary. This new title and designation was later shortened to Palaestina as, from which the modern, anglicized "Palestine" is derived."[105] The name "Falastin" that Arabs today use for "Palestine" is not an Arabic name, but is the Arab pronunciation of the Roman "Palaestina".

This was perhaps the first, but not the last, attempt to re-document the ownership of the Jewish Holy Lands, as is discussed earlier in this book in reference to similar attempts by Palestinian academicians. See the Fatwa in Appendix J which tries to justify other Islamic arguments that the Canaanites had a stronger claim to Palestine than the Jews and that the Jews lost their rights by refusing Islamic monotheism.

It is indisputable that the Jews lived and inhabited this land for thousands of years. Theirs was a strong and an independent state. Who amongst us has not heard of King David? And who amongst us has not heard of King Solomon and the magnificence of his kingdom? These were Jews and sons of Israel, the inhabitants of so-called Palestine. They were the rulers of this land and this country for over a thousand years in one stretch, and though they were exiled at several points in history, they returned back from these exiles again and again, and now they have been returned back to their land known as Israel and not Palestine.

Qur'anic reference credits the "land" to the Jews then takes it back!

Despite the Islamic doctrines and the convoluted interpretations of the Qur'anic passage of Sura 5:20 – 21 as explained earlier, and substantiated in Appendix B, according to the Islamic belief, Jacob (Yacoob) built a Mosque on the Temple Mount site. This was later renewed and rebuilt by King Solomon. This too was not a Jewish temple, but a mosque as all Jewish prophets were Muslims. Incidentally, King Solomon is recognized

---

[105] In http://www.palestinefacts.org/pf_early_palestine_name_origin.php, it states, "In AD 135, after putting down the Bar Kochba revolt, the second major Jewish revolt against Rome, the Emperor Hadrian wanted to blot out the name of the Roman 'Provincia Judaea' and so renamed it 'Provincia Syria Palaestina,' the Latin version of the Greek name and the first use of the name as an administrative unit. The name 'Provincia Syria Palaestina' was later shortened to Palaestina, from which the modern, anglicized 'Palestine' is derived."

in Islam as one of the prophets (being Muslim, of course). Furthermore, the true worshippers were the followers of Muslim Moses and Muslim Isa (Jesus). When the Jews rebelled and were no longer following the Islamic faith handed to them by their prophets Allah revoked the promise, removed the land from their possession and gave it to the Muslims.

> **Unbeknown to the Jews, the "promise" of the land was taken back before it was given!**
>
> Sura 5:20-21 *"And when Musa said to his people: O my people! remember the favour of Allah upon you when He raised prophets among you and made you kings and gave you what He had not given to any other among the nations. O my people! enter the holy land which Allah has prescribed for you and turn not on your backs for then you will turn back losers."*
>
> See text for why Allah revoked this "promise" according to Islamic sources.

Thus, according to various Islamic Fatwas, it is reckoned that land was originally given to the Jews but it is no longer theirs. However, the point we are making here is that despite the convoluted logic the Qur'an states that Allah had apportioned this land to the Jews. Being caught in their own web of contradictions it was natural to justify the Islamic position with an absurd logic. It is in the Qur'an that the land was given to the Jews thousands of years before the Arabs as reported in the Qur'an in the following Sura:

Sura 5:20-21 *"And when Musa said to his people: O my people! remember the favour of Allah upon you when He raised prophets among you and made you kings and gave you what He had not given to any other among the nations. O my people! enter the holy land which Allah has prescribed for you and turn not on your backs for then you will turn back losers."*

So, who then inhabited the land, the so-called land of Palestine first? The Jews, or the Muslims? On which historical criteria have the proponents of the Arab-Muslim rights based their judgment for promoting the rights of Arab Muslims above that of the Jews?

Who should one believe, the Qur'an and Islamic unattested claims, or the Biblical and the historical data, verified by the substantial historical and archaeological records?

Do the Muslims have any other proof for their right over Jerusalem apart from a disputed vision (the alleged rapture in the Israa' Wal Mi'raaj) or night dream mentioned in one remote verse of the Qur'an (Sura 17:1), and the reference in the Hadith which was made two hundred years later?[106]

The eye of the storm: A summation

Having established the retroactive Islamic claim to Monotheism, the logical and essential outworking was for Muhammad to apply this claim on several fronts, as we have tried to elaborate in this book.

The central doctrinal principle was to fully ignore the very existence of Judaism or Christianity as "religions" per se, but to recognize Jews and Christians only as members of Jewish or Christian communities respectively—communities who were "custodians" not owners of the original revelations and thus were guilty of having corrupted what was given to their patriarchs and prophets (including Moses and Jesus).

Practically, this dubious line of "reasoning" necessitated the "Muslim-hood" of the patriarchs and prophets and the appropriation of the birth-place of the Judeo-Christian monotheism—that being the Holy Land as a whole, and in particular, Jerusalem.

Thus to complete this deception, proof was needed. The Isra' wal Mi'raaj served that purpose. Through this vision and the doctrines built upon it in the ensuing 200-250 years, Islam has laid official claim to the Allah-given ownership of these lands, with a focal emphasis on Jerusalem as an Islamic "Waqf" nullifying and replacing all previous claims and thus establishing a non-augmentable doctrine of Islam—the obligation[107] on every member of the Muslim Ummah, wherever they may be, to "defend" this Waqf against the "usurpers," i.e. Jews and Christians.

That is why Jerusalem is now the "eye of the storm." The defence of the Islamic position is not only through the proclamations of Hamas, Hizbullah or the Islamic government of Iran, but is an academic and intel-

---

[106] The following appendices provided details of Fatwa's and other opinions regarding Jerusalem: Appendices B, C, G, H, I, J, K, and L.

[107] This is termed as a "Fard" in Arabic, i.e. a divine order imposed on all Muslims.

lectual battle on every campus in the US and Europe, as well as the rest of the world—as pro-Islamic academicians try to verify Islamic claims that the Jews have no currently valid claims, not even to the archaeological reality of an ongoing Jewish civilization up until today.

chapter 7
Summation and Closing Arguments

The re-framing of the problem

We started out saying that in approaching the issue of Islamic "enmity" toward the Jews—and thus to Israel—and ultimately to the "Other", we were not going to go into all of the ins and outs of the Arab-Israeli conflict, but instead were going to focus only on the root of that enmity and thus adhere to the Einsteinian principle that the definition and proper framing of a problem must precede any attempts at formulating solutions.

Einstein is famously quoted as having said, "*If I had one hour to save the world, I would spend fifty-five minutes defining the problem, and only five minutes finding the solution.*" Because the quality of the solutions one comes up with will be in direct proportion to the quality of the description of the problem one is trying to solve. In other words, "the problem is to know what the problem is!"

We believe we have done that in this book. We have provided the social background and set the political and/or social context. Then we have defined the problem by posing rhetorical questions critical of the key political solution currently on the table—the "Two-State" solution—which we view as incorrectly framing the question by inverting the "cause" and the "effect", and so obscuring the issue by providing a smokescreen for the true Islamic intent.

But we have not deviated from the other more important self-imposed constraint NOT to propose any solutions, but just to fill in the details necessary to be able to determine the true cause, or origin, of the Islamic "enmity" toward the Jews, as well as the true cause of the conflict over the "land"—both of which are obscured to outsiders by the rhetorical and intentional illusion that Israel is causing the enmity by her actions.

In the process we have also presented you with an accurate perspective of the grip that the Islamic source books have on the thoughts and behaviour of the individual Muslim, as well as the Muslim society at large and Islamic policy. In this pursuit, we believe that we have managed to stay true to our self-imposed constraints, and have endeavoured to lay out for you in simple and understandable terms (in so far as the difficult material will allow) those doctrines within the Qur'an as supported by the example of Muhammad in the Sunnah, and maintained by the various generations of Islamic scholars. Thus we have remained steadily on course in laying out the Islamic doctrines behind all of the critical and linked aspects of the problem.

This exposition of the problem has been a long and meticulous exercise in controlled inductive reasoning, in explaining the almost unexplainable, and now in approaching the bottom line we remind you of the key questions we have endeavoured to answer:

- What is the root of "enmity" toward the Jews within the Islamic sources?

- How is it really tied to the "land" issues?

- How does the answer to the first two questions impact the framing of the current Palestinian-Israeli conflict?

- And, just what is the bottom line, after all is said and done?

To get there, we must go through a concise summation of what we have presented, and we believe—established, well beyond a reasonable doubt.

Adding it all up…!

In the foregoing it has been shown and fully documented from the primary Islamic sources (the Qur'an, the Sunnah and the biography of Muhammad, the Sira), that the Islamic enmity towards the Jews, and thus to modern Israel, is profoundly Qur'anic, inspired by Allah as claimed by

Muhammad. But that is not the end of it—we have pressed further to determine: What was the cause of such deep-seated enmity as we have uncovered in the Qur'an? What could the Jews have done to Muhammad or the Muslims at a point in history when he had just announced his mission?

And yet the enmity did start exactly at that point. We have shown from within these primary Islamic sources that once Muhammad announced his "mission" in Mecca to "bring back Monotheism" to the Arabian peninsula—the die was cast that his retroactive claim to the Islamic origin of "monotheism", the doctrine of Fitrah, would be in direct and mortal conflict with the previous "revelations" by the Jewish Patriarchs as well as the Christian Apostles, including Jesus, and thus is the inescapable motive for "enmity" toward those to whom the true original revelations had been given.

Ironically, Muhammad's claim to the origin of pure "Islamic monotheism" was seriously misunderstood by many of the Jews and Christians of the time as being a claim to a distinctive "Islamic" form of monotheism—a type of "reform" as per his self-proclaimed initial title as the "Warner." Even many today regard Islam to have been a mission to bring the pagans of Arabia into the fold of the established monotheism. However, it was never that, as we have shown, but was always meant to be a claim that Islamic monotheism predated the Judeo-Christian monotheism, and that there was never such a thing as "Judaism" or "Christianity" but only the people called Jews and Christians. As explained earlier, even they were all Muslims.

Hence, from that day on, Muhammad's remaining tasks were clear. It became essential, having claimed the roots of Judeo-Christian Monotheism itself, to re-direct the earlier revelations in order to support this claim. He accomplished this by retro-actively declaring all mankind to have also been Muslim by nature from the time of Adam, and proclaiming all the former prophets, including Jesus, to have been created "neither Jew nor Christian, but Muslim." At the same time he disenfranchised all those rank and file Jews and Christians of previous centuries as reported in the Torah and the New Testament, those to whom the earlier revelations had been given, by relegating them to the subservient station of having been "only the custodians" of the earlier "Islamic" revelations of the "one god, Allah", and unfaithful custodians at that.

Thus the only positive recognition he gave to both Jew and Christian was to assign to them the temporary role of "custodians" of the first revelations (see tablet in figure 1), and as a consequence he assigned them the dubious and double-edged "honor" and "curse" of being only the "People of the Book"—but unfaithful recipients of the revelations—with strict regulations and severely curtailed rights within Muslim society. At the same time he simultaneously charged them with having changed the scriptures under their care by removing references to himself as the "Seal of the Prophets" and thus bringing down Allah's permanent wrath upon themselves.

Added to the foregoing we have also shown that the references in the Qur'an and the Sunnah which made both explicit and implicit allusions to this enmity, were and are couched in such duplicitous terms that they can be read and used as either positive or negative so that the negative meanings pass undetected or can be rationalized away by the un-initiated. As a result, the Jews and the Christians of that day were totally unaware and uninformed of the reality of the lethal meaning behind these allusions to their character and their standing before Allah. Though they could see through the forgery his false claims and factual errors in the various narratives and theology they remained basically innocent in regard to the more outrageous claims concerning the appropriation of their own scriptures as well as the curses that were being hurled at them daily.

It was within this neutral or apparently congenial climate with the Jews and the Christians, and while still in Mecca but preparing to immigrate to the primarily Jewish city of Yathrib, that Muhammad "suddenly" experienced the supernatural journey from Mecca to the Temple Mount and beyond—that we have shown is the basis for the "Waqf," which you will recall is Allah's endowment to the Muslim Ummah to permanently lay official claim to Jerusalem and the entire Holy Land. At the time this vision was considered to be controversial, but over time became more and more accepted to the point that some 200 years later it was made into law.

Therefore we see that Muhammad had already established theological grounds for the origin of Islamic monotheism during his mission in Mecca, thus necessitating the permanent enmity toward the Jews (and Christians).

But virtually on the eve of the Hijra to Yathrib, he suddenly established claim to Jerusalem, the birthplace of Judeo-Christian monotheism—while secretly and concurrently initiating the political steps necessary for the eventual elimination of Jews (and Christians) from Arabia.

Therefore, although conceived in Mecca, this Allah-based "enmity" and resulting "wrath" was first enforced in Yathrib/Medina—so after a brief interlude, or "honeymoon" period with the Jews of that city, he gave them the first ultimatum, convert or face the sword. Poetically, under the self-termed doctrine of "assumed enmity", a policy of pre-emptive self-defence coined and institutionalized by Muhammad, he acted in all brutality and utter cruelty, in completely cleansing the city of the three indigenous Jewish tribes within the first three years after the Hijra when they refused to accept him as the "praised one" predicted in their scriptures as per his claim.

Therefore, starting with the exiling of Banu Kaynuka and Banu Nadir and the merciless slaughter of the men of Banu Qurayza in April, 627 A.D. as a first step in defining his policy toward the Jews—in one fell swoop, the Jews who had founded and made Yathrib thrive were no more, leaving their city to be known henceforth singularly as Medina, the purely Islamic second holiest city of the new religion, and the first capital of the newly constituted political entity—the Islamic Caliphate.

The next step and another milestone in establishing and completing the Islamic policy toward the Jews (and later Christians) came shortly thereafter with the attack, defeat and enslaving of the Jews of Khaybar in March, 628 A.D., another primarily Jewish city—through the application of what is now known as the "Doctrine of Dhimmitude", that consolidated and institutionalized Islamic enmity as a legitimate bone fide and enforceable component of Islam and its teachings, as well as it's legal code of governance.

Now the stage was set for the emergence of Muhammad and Islam as a world power. His intermediate steps remained to bring Jews and Christians of Arabia under this new form of governance, called "Dhimmitude" prior to laying the groundwork for ridding the entirety of Arabia of the Jewish and Christian presence. But now the policies of a type of "containment" for non-Muslims was in place, such that as the Islamic armies spread out of Arabia the conquered peoples- Jews and Christians were given three choices—convert, Dhimmitude, or the sword.

If this is true, then…?

Skipping ahead some 14 centuries, we submit that this is the framework within which the current Muslim-Jewish conflict should be viewed— as it is currently playing itself out on the world stage under the label of the Palestinian-Israeli conflict. We have established, however, that this conflict is neither a Palestinian-Israeli conflict nor an Arab-Israeli conflict, but is rather a Muslim-Jewish conflict.

The present day "enmity" between the Palestinians and the Israelis which is popularly thought to emanate solely from the dispute over the "land" in a secular sense of a normally displaced people group (or population shift or exchange), can instead now be seen for what it is—the result of Islamic enmity toward the Jews in general, and magnified in particular because of their being on what Muslims claim as the "Islamic Waqf", or land which has been set aside eternally as Islamic property reserved only for the Muslim Ummah as explained in detail in the body of the text.

With this in mind, we have established that the conflict over the "land" between Palestine and the State of Israel is NOT a localized political conflict solely between the Israeli and Palestinian people over the land, which could be solved by the compromise of a Two-State solution. Instead it can better be seen as a policy decision by Muslim leaders to provide a "smokescreen" of misinformation to justify and obscure the Islamic hate concealed within the pages of the Qur'an and the Sunnah.

Hence the myth that Israel has caused the enmity can also be seen for what it is—a distortion of "cause and effect" meant to distract from the true roots of both the endemic Islamic "enmity" toward the Jews, and the endemic Islamic "claims" to Jerusalem and the entire Holy Land.

Consequently, we have answered a key apparently outrageous rhetorical question as previously posed—that even if a Two-State solution were established in the Holy Land, it would sooner or later run up against the mandates in the Qur'an and Sunnah and face a similar plight—or hypothetically in another scenario, if Israel were transported to another spot on the globe, the mandates against the existence of Jews would still be in force no matter where they might be. In fact this happened originally at the birth of Islam, when Arabia was completely cleansed of Jews (and Christians).

Similarly in today's world this "enmity", is currently being taught to Muslims everywhere including host countries in the West—repeating and affirming those vile and abusive Qur'anic descriptions of the Jew's character and intent—which are being held as truth by a new generation of young people. This trend does not bode well, but instead provides a substantial obstacle to forming peaceful relations in the future between Muslims and Jews—an obstacle that is insurmountable.

Is there a bottom line?

In the opening chapter of this book, "Setting the Context: The Search for the Bottom Line," we stated that this book relates to one basic, but emerging theme: The 7th century origins of Islamic enmity to the Jews commencing with Muhammad's announcement of his mission to correct and complete the "Judeo-Christian" revelations, and thus in his eyes, go back to "restore" Islamic Monotheism—with its continuing implications to the current Arab-Israeli conflict in the Middle East, and beyond to the wider global context.

We have identified that source as amply described in the book, and in the foregoing summation, but more importantly, we have also identified the underlying motive for that "enmity"—which has a more far reaching implication—one that has been virtually hidden or obscured, denied or conveniently ignored from the perspective of the western world for many diverse reasons. The West was deeply engrossed with its own battles coming from all quarters, e.g. the Reformation, the Renaissance, the discovery of the New World, scrambling for colonies, the Industrial Revolution, etc. During these times the West, for its own ends reached a liveable, workable agreement with the Muslim hierarchy, who in turn were jockeying for favour with the new regimes.

Hence the vast masses in the West remained untouched and unaffected for centuries in regard to a realistic recognition of the significance of Islam and what was going on thousands of miles away.

However, in today's global village this significance is increasingly being recognized. As post-colonial mainstream Islam has been on the rise, indeed in resurgence, inside Muslim-majority countries and in the Western world during the last several decades, it is being exposed as it reasserts its power and control in modern society. Hence the furore over adopting international laws to prevent any form of scrutiny or criticism of Islam, under the guise of preventing "the defamation of religions," as Islam cannot bear scrutiny.

The Inevitable Conclusion

The inevitable conclusion is that each of these doctrines work together to establish the Muslim Ummah as being set apart by Allah and his messenger from the beginning of time. The Ummah is cut from a different cloth from the rest of humanity, having extra "rights" vis-a-vis the other members of society, extra rewards, and extra "land", i.e. ultimately the entire world as a "mosque." Thus, all belongs to Islam, by way of dominion through the leadership of its messenger Muhammad.

The Islamic concepts of Fitrah, the Muslim DNA of all mankind, the Muslimhood of all prophets and the Jewish patriarchs, the linking of Tawheed (the Islamic version of monotheism) with the doctrine of Al-Walaa' wa Al-Baraa' (Allegiance and Rejection), and the Isra' wal Mi'raaj (Night Journey) together consolidate the totality of Islamic claims, especially against the Jews.

The book itself has been organized as an inferential journey through the high points of the narrative of the first advent of Islam, focusing on Muhammad's own definition of his mission, which can be seen from the perspective of history as a systematic removal and replacement of key doctrines in order to validate his prophethood as the Seal of the Prophets and his priesthood as the only legitimate intercessor between Allah and mankind. These taken together constitute Islam's appropriation of the entire Jewish and Christian belief system, plus their claims to the Holy Land, without any real, viable, historical, logical foundation. Thus the total fallacy of Islam rooted in its doctrine of enmity is exposed, and its entire edifice is threatened.

Appendix A
Details of Qur'anic Text on Portrayal of Jews

In what follows we provide the detailed text of the Sura's on the portrayal of the Jews as provided in Chapter 3.

A. Allah's key charges and judgments against the Jews (and Christians) (selected):

- Sura 9:30, Jews associated a son (Ezra) to Allah..." (Shirk, i.e. polytheism)

  "The Jews call 'Uzair a son of Allah, and the Christians call Christ the son of Allah. That is a saying from their mouth; (in this) they but imitate what the unbelievers of old used to say. Allah's curse be on them: how they are deluded away from the Truth!" (Yusuf Ali)

- Sura 7:138, "Jews were calf worshippers..." (Idol worshippers)

  "We took the Children of Israel (with safety) across the sea. They came upon a people devoted entirely to some idols they had. They said: "O Moses! fashion for us a god like unto the gods they have." He said: "Surely ye are a people without knowledge." (Yusuf Ali)

- Sura 9:31,"Jews took their leaders as gods instead of Allah..." (Shirk, i.e. polytheism)

  "They take their priests and their anchorites to be their lords in derogation of Allah, and (they take as their Lord) Christ the son of Mary; yet they were commanded to worship but

One Allah: there is no god but He. Praise and glory to Him: (Far is He) from having the partners they associate (with Him)." (Yusuf Ali)

- Sura 5:64, Sura 3:181, "Jews reproached Allah…" (In rebellion against Allah)

  5:64 *"The Jews say: "Allah's hand is tied up." Be their hands tied up and be they accursed for the (blasphemy) they utter. Nay, both His hands are widely outstretched: He giveth and spendeth (of His bounty) as He pleaseth. But the revelation that cometh to thee from Allah increaseth in most of them their obstinate rebellion and blasphemy. Amongst them we have placed enmity and hatred till the Day of Judgment. Every time they kindle the fire of war, Allah doth extinguish it; but they (ever) strive to do mischief on earth. And Allah loveth not those who do mischief."* (Yusuf Ali)

  3:181 *"Allah hath heard the taunt of those who say: "Truly, Allah is indigent and we are rich!"- We shall certainly record their word and (their act) of slaying the prophets in defiance of right, and We shall say: "Taste ye the penalty of the Scorching Fire!"* (Yusuf Ali)

- Sura 2:87, Sura 5:70, " the Jews are prophet killers…" (In rebellion)

  2:87 *"We gave Moses the Book and followed him up with a succession of messengers; We gave Jesus the son of Mary Clear (Signs) and strengthened him with the holy spirit. Is it that whenever there comes to you a messenger with what ye yourselves desire not, ye are puffed up with pride?- Some ye called impostors, and others ye slay!"* (Yusuf Ali)

  5:70 *"We took the covenant of the Children of Israel and sent them messengers, every time, there came to them a messenger with what they themselves desired not - some (of these) they called impostors, and some they (go so far as to) slay."* (Yusuf Ali)

- Sura 2:100, Sura 5:13," Jews are covenant breakers, full of treason, vengeful…" (In rebellion)

  2:100 *"Is it not (the case) that every time they make a covenant, some party among them throw it aside?- Nay, Most of them are faithless."* (Yusuf Ali)

  5:13 *"But because of their breach of their covenant, We cursed them, and made their hearts grow hard; they change the words from their (right) places and forget a good part of the message that was sent them, nor wilt thou cease to find them- barring a few - ever bent on (new) deceits: but forgive them, and overlook (their misdeeds): for Allah loveth those who are kind."* (Yusuf Ali)

- Sura 5:79," the Jews made lawful all that was forbidden…" (Rebellion, Lawless People)

  "They used not to forbid one another from the Munkar (wrong, evil-doing, sins, polytheism, disbelief, etc.) which they committed. Vile indeed was what they used to do." (Al-Hilali)

- Sura 4:51-52, "Jews practicing sorcery and witchcraft…" (Evildoers)

  "51 Hast thou not turned Thy vision to those who were given a portion of the Book? they believe in sorcery and Evil, and say to the Unbelievers that they are better guided in the (right) way Than the believers! 52 They are (men) whom Allah hath cursed: And those whom Allah Hath cursed, thou wilt find, have no one to help." (Yusuf Ali)

- Sura 5:64, "Jews are igniters of fires of war…" (Rebellion, Lawless People)

  "The Jews say: "Allah's hand is tied up." Be their hands tied up and be they accursed for the (blasphemy) they utter. Nay, both His hands are widely outstretched: He giveth and spendeth (of His bounty) as He pleaseth. But the revelation that cometh to thee from Allah increaseth in most of them

their obstinate rebellion and blasphemy. Amongst them we have placed enmity and hatred till the Day of Judgment. Every time they kindle the fire of war, Allah doth extinguish it; but they (ever) strive to do mischief on earth. And Allah loveth not those who do mischief." (Yusuf Ali)

- Sura 5:62, 17:4, "Jews are corrupters on earth,…" (Rebellion, Lawless People)

  5:62 "*Many of them dost thou see, racing each other in sin and rancour, and their eating of things forbidden. Evil indeed are the things that they do.*" (Yusuf Ali)

  17:4 "*And We gave (Clear) Warning to the Children of Israel in the Book, that twice would they do mischief on the earth and be elated with mighty arrogance (and twice would they be punished)!*" (Yusuf Ali)

- Sura 2:75, Sura 4:46, "The Jews corrupted the scriptures…" (Corruptors of scriptures)

  2:75 "*Can ye (o ye men of Faith) entertain the hope that they will believe in you?- Seeing that a party of them heard the Word of Allah, and perverted it knowingly after they understood it.*" (Yusuf Ali)

  4:46 "*Of the Jews there are those who displace words from their (right) places, and say: 'We hear and we disobey'; and 'Hear what is not Heard'; and 'Ra'ina'; with a twist of their tongues and a slander to Faith. If only they had said: 'What hear and we obey'; and 'Do hear'; and "Do look at us"; it would have been better for them, and more proper; but Allah hath cursed them for their Unbelief; and but few of them will believe.*" (Yusuf Ali)

- Sura 2:42, "Jews conceal truth with falsehood,…" (Corruptors of scriptures)

  "*And cover not Truth with falsehood, nor conceal the Truth when ye know (what it is).*" (Yusuf Ali)

- Sura 9:32, "Jews tried to extinguish Allah's light..." (Corruptors of scriptures)

  "They (the disbelievers, the Jews and the Christians) want to extinguish Allâh's Light (with which Muhammad SAW has been sent - Islâmic Monotheism) with their mouths, but Allâh will not allow except that His Light should be perfected even though the Kâfirûn (disbelievers) hate (it)." (Al-Hilali)

- Sura 3:183-184, "Jews are liars..." (Immoral character)

  "183 Those (Jews) who said: "Verily, Allâh has taken our promise not to believe in any Messenger unless he brings to us an offering which the fire (from heaven) shall devour." Say: "Verily, there came to you Messengers before me, with clear signs and even with what you speak of; why then did you kill them, if you are truthful?" 184 Then if they reject you (O Muhammad SAW), so were Messengers rejected before you, who came with Al-Baiyinât (clear signs, proofs, evidences) and the Scripture and the Book of Enlightenment." (Al-Hilali)

- Sura 2:93-96, "Jews are cowards, protective of their lives, they don't fight except from behind fortresses..." (Immoral character)

  "93 And (remember) when We took your covenant and We raised above you the Mount (saying), "Hold firmly to what We have given you and hear (Our Word). They said, "We have heard and disobeyed." And their hearts absorbed (the worship of) the calf because of their disbelief. Say: "Worst indeed is that which your faith enjoins on you if you are believers." 94 Say to (them): "If the home of the Hereafter with Allâh is indeed for you specially and not for others, of mankind, then long for death if you are truthful." 95 But they will never long for it because of what their hands have sent before them (i.e. what they have done). And Allâh is All-Aware of the Zâlimûn (polytheists and wrong-doers). 96

And verily, you will find them (the Jews) the greediest of mankind for life and (even greedier) than those who - ascribe partners to Allâh (and do not believe in Resurrection - Magians, pagans, and idolaters, etc.). Everyone of them wishes that he could be given a life of a thousand years. But the grant of such life will not save him even a little from (due) punishment. And Allâh is All-Seer of what they do." (Al-Hialali)

● Sura 4:161, "Jews are devourers and chargers of usury..." (Immoral character)

"And their taking of Ribâ (usury) though they were forbidden from taking it and their devouring of men's substance wrongfully (bribery, etc.). And We have prepared for the disbelievers among them a painful torment." (Al-Hilali)

● Sura 5:62, "Jews are lovers of transgression and sin..." (Immoral character)

"Many of them dost thou see, racing each other in sin and rancour, and their eating of things forbidden. Evil indeed are the things that they do." (Yusuf Ali)

● Sura 2:142, "Jews are vulgar and fools..." (Immoral character)

"The fools among the people will say: "What hath turned them from the Qibla to which they were used?" Say: To Allah belong both east and West: He guideth whom He will to a Way that is straight." (Yusuf Ali)

● Sura 5:64, "Jews are haters of one another and full of enmity to their own..." (Immoral character)

"The Jews say: "Allah's hand is tied up." Be their hands tied up and be they accursed for the (blasphemy) they utter. Nay, both His hands are widely outstretched: He giveth and spendeth (of His bounty) as He pleaseth. But the revelation that cometh to thee from Allah increaseth in most of them their obstinate rebellion and blasphemy. Amongst them we

have placed enmity and hatred till the Day of Judgment. Every time they kindle the fire of war, Allah doth extinguish it; but they (ever) strive to do mischief on earth. And Allah loveth not those who do mischief." (Yusuf Ali)

- Sura 2:145, Sura 7:132, "Jews are hard hearted..." (Irredeemable hearts)

   2:145 *"Even if thou wert to bring to the people of the Book all the Signs (together), they would not follow Thy Qibla; nor art thou going to follow their Qibla; nor indeed will they follow each other's Qibla. If thou after the knowledge hath reached thee, Wert to follow their (vain) desires,-then wert thou Indeed (clearly) in the wrong."* (Yusuf Ali)

   7:132 *"They said (to Moses): "Whatever be the Signs thou bringest, to work therewith thy sorcery on us, we shall never believe in thee."* (Yusuf Ali)

- Sura 2:74, 88, " Jews' hearts are harder then stones..." (Irredeemable hearts)

   2:74 *"Thenceforth were your hearts hardened: They became like a rock and even worse in hardness. For among rocks there are some from which rivers gush forth; others there are which when split asunder send forth water; and others which sink for fear of Allah. And Allah is not unmindful of what ye do."* (Yusuf Ali)

   2:88 *"They say, "Our hearts are the wrappings (which preserve Allah's Word: we need no more)." Nay, Allah's curse is on them for their blasphemy: Little is it they believe."* (Yusuf Ali)

B. Allah's judgments, curses and penalties against the Jews (selected):
   - Sura 1:7, "Jews are people on whom is the wrath of Allah," (Cursed by Allah)

      "The Way of those on whom You have bestowed Your Grace

not *(the way) of those who earned Your Anger (such as the Jews), nor of those who went astray (such as the Christians)."* (Al-Hilali)

- Sura 4:51-52, "...whosoever is cursed by Allah will find himself no helper..." (Rejection of Muslims and therefore, cursed by Allah)

  "51 Have you not seen those who were given a portion of the Scripture? They believe in Jibt and Tâghût and say to the disbelievers that they are better guided as regards the way than the believers (Muslims). 52 They are those whom Allâh has cursed, and he whom Allâh curses, you will not find for him (any) helper," (Al-Hilali)

- Sura 7:152, Jews deserve "...wrath from their Lord and humiliation will come upon them..." (Cursed by Allah)

  "Certainly, those who took the calf (for worship), wrath from their Lord and humiliation will come upon them in the life of this world. Thus do We recompense those who invent lies." (Al-Hilali)

- Sura 58:14, The Jews are "...a people upon whom is the wrath of Allâh..." (Cursed by Allah)

  "Have you (O Muhammad SAW) not seen those (hypocrites) who take for friends a people upon whom is the Wrath of Allâh (i.e. Jews)? They are neither of you (Muslims) nor of them (Jews), and they swear to a lie while they know." (Al-Hilali)

- Sura 2:65, 5:60, 7:166, "Jews are those who were cursed and transformed into apes and swine..." (Cursed and judged by Allah)

  2:65 *"And indeed you knew those amongst you who transgressed in the matter of the Sabbath (i.e. Saturday). We said to them: "Be you monkeys, despised and rejected."* (Al-Hilali)

5:60 *"Say (O Muhammad SAW to the people of the Scripture):* *"Shall I inform you of something worse than that, regarding the recompense from Allâh: those (Jews) who incurred the Curse of Allâh and His Wrath, those of whom (some) He transformed into monkeys and swines, those who worshipped Tâghût (false deities); such are worse in rank (on the Day of Resurrection in the Hell-fire), and far more astray from the Right Path (in the life of this world)."* (Al-Hilali)

7:166 *"So when they exceeded the limits of what they were prohibited, We said to them: "Be you monkeys, despised and rejected." (It is a severe warning to the mankind that they should not disobey what Allâh commands them to do, and be far away from what He prohibits them)."* (Al-Hilali)

● Sura 2:61, Sura 3:112, "…they drew on themselves the Wrath of Allâh…because they used to disbelieve the proofs…" (Cursed and judged by Allah)

2:61 *"And (remember) when you said, "O Mûsa (Moses)! We cannot endure one kind of food. So invoke your Lord for us to bring forth for us of what the earth grows, its herbs, its cucumbers, its Fûm (wheat or garlic), its lentils and its onions." He said, "Would you exchange that which is better for that which is lower? Go you down to any town and you shall find what you want!" And they were covered with humiliation and misery, and they drew on themselves the Wrath of Allâh. That was because they used to disbelieve the Ayât (proofs, evidences, verses, lessons, signs, revelations, etc.) of Allâh and killed the Prophets wrongfully. That was because they disobeyed and used to transgress the bounds (in their disobedience to Allâh, i.e. commit crimes and sins)."* (Al-Hilali)

3:112 *"Indignity is put over them wherever they may be, except when under a covenant (of protection) from Allâh, and from men; they have drawn on themselves the Wrath of*

Allâh, and destruction is put over them. This is because they disbelieved in the Ayât (proofs, evidences, verses, lessons, signs, revelations, etc.) of Allâh and killed the Prophets without right. This is because they disobeyed (Allâh) and used to transgress beyond bounds (in Allâh's disobedience, crimes and sins)." (Al-Hilali)

- Sura 8:55- 56, 98:6, " Jews are the worst of Allah's creation…" (Allah final judgment)

  8:55-56 *"55 For the worst of beasts in the sight of Allah are those who reject Him: They will not believe. 56 They are those with whom thou didst make a covenant, but they break their covenant every time, and they have not the fear (of Allah)."* (Yusuf Ali)

  98:6 *"Those who reject (Truth), among the People of the Book and among the Polytheists, will be in Hell-Fire, to dwell therein (for aye). They are the worst of creatures."* (Yusuf Ali)

Appendix B
Islamic Scholar's Commentary on Islam's Right to Jerusalem[108]

(Authors' comment: The following is response to the question whereby the questioner sees that the Jews have a legitimate stake in Jerusalem, but whereby the responder, a top Islamic authority vehemently and "systematically" builds the Islamic argument that even if the Jews had some presence in the holy land, they had forfeited any and all rights because of their "unbelief" And hence, Jerusalem should be 100% an Islamic property forever).

Q uestion: As a Muslim, I am always told that the city of Jerusalem is important to us. But why? I am aware that Prophet Yaqoob (Jacob) built the Aqsa Mosque in it and that Prophet Muhammad (p.b.u.h) led the previous Prophets in prayer signifying the unity of the message and all divine revelations, is there any other major reason or is it just because it is that we are dealing with Jews. It seems to me that the Jews have more stake to it.

Response by Islamic Scholar: Sheikh Muhammed Salih Al-Munajjid[109]

- Allaah has described it in the Qur'aan as being blessed. He said (interpretation of the meaning): "Glorified (and Exalted) be He

---

[108] Islam Q&A: http://islamqa.com/en/ref/7726/bayt%20al%20maqdis
[109] The responder is a top Islamic authority in Saudi Arabia.

(Allaah) Who took His slave (Muhammad) for a journey by night from Al-Masjid Al-Haraam (at Makkah) to Al-Masjid Al-Aqsaa (in Jerusalem), the neighbourhood whereof We have blessed..." [al-Israa' 17:1]. Al-Quds is part of the neighbourhood surrounding the mosque and hence it is blessed.

- Allaah has described it as being holy, as He says (interpretation of the meaning): "[Moosa said:] O my people! Enter the holy land (Palestine) which Allaah has assigned to you..." [al-Maa'idah 5:21]

- In al-Quds there is al-Masjid al-Aqsaa, and one prayer there is equivalent to two hundred and fifty prayers elsewhere.

It was reported that Abu Dharr (may Allaah be pleased with him) said: we were discussing, in the presence of the Prophet (peace and blessings of Allaah be upon him), which of them was more virtuous, the mosque of the Messenger of Allaah (peace and blessings of Allaah be upon him) or Bayt al-Maqdis. The Messenger of Allaah (peace and blessings of Allaah be upon him) said: One prayer in my mosque is better than four prayers there, but it is still a good place of prayer. Soon there will come a time when if a man has a spot of land as big as his horse's rope from which he can see Bayt al-Maqdis, that will be better for him than the whole world. (Narrated and classed as saheeh by al-Haakim, 4/509. Al-Dhahabi and al-Albaani agreed with him, as stated in al-Silsilah al-Saheehah, at the end of the discussion of Hadith no. 2902).

One prayer in al-Masjid al-Nabawi is equivalent to one thousand prayers elsewhere, so one prayer in al-Masjid al-Aqsaa is equivalent to two hundred and fifty prayers elsewhere.

With regard to the famous Hadith which says that prayer in al-Masjid al-Aqsaa is equivalent to five hundred prayers elsewhere, this is da'eef (weak). (See Tamaam al-Minnah [?] by Shaykh al-Albaani – may Allaah have mercy on him – p. 292).

- The one-eyed Dajjaal ("Antichrist") will not enter it, because of the Hadith, "He will prevail over all the earth, apart from al-Haram [in Makkah] and Bayt al-Maqdis." (Narrated by Ahmad, 19665. Classed as saheeh by Ibn Khuzaymah, 2/327, and Ibn Hibbaan, 7/102).

- The Dajjaal will be killed close to al-Quds. He will be killed by the Messiah 'Eesa ibn Maryam (peace be upon him), as was stated in the Hadith: "The son of Maryam will kill the Dajjaal at the gates of Ludd." (Narrated by Muslim, 2937, from the Hadith of al-Nawwaas ibn Sam'aan). Ludd (Lod) is a place near Bayt al-Maqdis.

- The Messenger (peace and blessings of Allaah be upon him) was taken to Bayt al-Maqdis on his Night Journey (al-Israa') from al-Masjid al-Haraam to al-Masjid al-Aqsaa. Allaah says (interpretation of the meaning): "Glorified (and Exalted) be He (Allaah) Who took His slave (Muhammad) for a journey by night from Al-Masjid Al-Haraam (at Makkah) to Al-Masjid Al-Aqsaa (in Jerusalem)..." [al-Israa' 17:1].

- It (al-Quds) was the first Qiblah of the Muslims, as was reported by al-Baraa' (may Allaah be pleased with him): the Messenger of Allaah (peace and blessings of Allaah be upon him) prayed in the direction of Bayt al-Maqdis for sixteen or seventeen months. (Narrated by al-Bukhari, 41 – this version was narrated by him – and by Muslim, 525).

- It is the place where Wahy (Revelation) came down, and it is the homeland of the Prophets. This is well known.

- It is one of the mosques to which people may travel.

Here we would caution readers against believing that the Jews, Christians and Muslims are following the same principles nowadays, because the Jews have changed the religion of their Prophet. Indeed, part of the religion of their Prophet is that they should follow our Prophet and not reject him, but they disbelieve in the Prophethood of Muhammad (peace and blessings of Allaah be upon him) and associate others in worship with Allaah.

The Jews do not have any stake in al-Quds, because even though they may have lived in the land previously, that land now belongs to the Muslims from two points of view:

1. The Jews disbelieved and are no longer following the religion of the believers among the Children of Israel who followed and supported Moosa and 'Eesaa (peace be upon them).

2. We Muslims have more right to it than them, because land does not belong to the people who lived there first, but to those who establish the laws of Allaah therein. Allaah created the land, and He created people to worship Allaah in the land and to establish therein the religion, laws and rulings of Allaah. Allaah says (interpretation of the meaning): "…Verily, the earth is Allaah's. He gives it as a heritage to whom He wills of His slaves; and the (blessed) end is for the Muttaqoon (the pious)." [al-A'raaf 7:128]

Hence if some Arabs came who were not followers of Islam and they ruled the land with kufr, they would have to be fought until they submitted to the rule of Islam or were killed. It is not the matter of race or ethnicity; it is the matter of Tawheed and Islam.

Appendix c
More Graphic Details about the Night Journey[110]

(Authors' Note: The following is another record of the events during Muhammad's alleged night journey. The significance of these details that are provided in the Hadith is that they provide a very graphic treatment of what Muhammad allegedly observed—details that are reminiscent of some eschatological writings in the Bible).

Hadith records on the night journey

This was also recorded by At-Tirmidhi, who said it is *Gharib* Ahmad also recorded that Anas said: "The Messenger of Allah said: 'When I was taken up to my Lord (during Al-Mi'raaj), I passed by people who had nails of copper with which they were scratching their faces and chests. I asked, 'Who are these, O Jibril' He said, 'These are those who ate the flesh of the people [i.e., backbiting] and slandered their honor'." This was also recorded by Abu Dawud.

Anas also said that the Messenger of Allah said: "On the night when I was taken on my Night Journey (Al-Isra'), I passed by Musa, who was standing, praying in his grave." This was also recorded by Muslim.

As such, there is scholarly consensus (ijma') Prophet Muhammad (P. B. B. U. H.) journeyed in BODY and SOUL on the night of al-Isra' from Masjid al-Haram in Makkah to Masjid al-Aqsa in Jerusalem. Moreover, the person who denies al-Isra' is a blasphemer for belying the manifest text of the Qur'an.

---

[110] http://www.chowrangi.com/al-isra-wal-miraj-the-night-journey-and-theascension-of-prophet-muhammad-peace-and-blessings-be-upon-him.html

Before the Prophet took this night journey, the ceiling of the house in which he was staying was opened, and Jibril descended. He cut open the chest of Prophet Muhammad and washed that open area with Zamzam water. Then he emptied something from a container into the chest of the Prophet to increase his wisdom as well as the strength of his belief. This was done to prepare the Messenger of Allah for that which he had yet to see in the upper world from among the wonders of the creation of Allah.

Imam Ahmad recorded that Anas bin Malik said that Malik bin Sasaah told him that the Prophet of Allah told them about the night in which he was taken on the Night Journey (Al-Isra'). He said:

"While I was lying down in Al-Hatim (or maybe, Qatadah said, in Al-Hijr) 'someone came to me and said to his companion, 'The one who is in the middle of these three.' He came to me and opened me." I [one of the narrators] heard Qatadah say, 'split me - from here to here.' Qatadah said: "I said to Al-Jarud, who was beside me, 'What does that mean' He said, 'From the top of his chest to below his navel', and I heard him say, 'from his throat to below his navel.'

The Prophet said:

"He took out my heart and brought a golden vessel filled with faith and wisdom. He washed my heart then filled it up and put it back, then a white animal was brought to me that was smaller than a mule and larger than a donkey."

Some of the things that the Muhammad (P. B. B. U. H.) saw on this Blessed Night are as follows:

1. Allah enabled the Prophet (P. B. B. U. H.) to see the world (dunya) like an old woman. However, this old woman was wearing a great deal of jewelry, and in this there is an indication signifying the reality of the world.

2. Allah enabled the Prophet (P. B. B. U. H.) to see Iblees. The Prophet (P. B. B. U. H.) saw something on the side of the road which did not dare to stand in his way or speak to him. What the Prophet saw was Iblees-e-La'een*.

3. On his journey, the Prophet P. B. B. U. H.) smelled a very nice odour. He asked Jibril (a.s.) about this pleasant scent and Jibril (a.s.) informed him this good smell was coming from the grave of the woman whose duty used to be to comb Pharaoh's daughter's hair. This woman was a good, pious believer. One day, as she was combing Pharaoh's daughter's hair, the comb fell from her hand. At this she said, "*Bismillah*". Pharaoh's daughter asked her, "Do you have a god other than my father?" The woman said, "Yes. My Lord and the Lord of your father is Allah." Pharaoh's daughter told her father what had happened. Pharaoh demanded this woman blaspheme and leave Islam, but she refused. At that, Pharaoh threatened to kill her children. He brought a great pot of water and built a great fire under it. When the water boiled, Pharaoh brought her children and started to drop them into that pot one after the other. Throughout all this, the woman remained steadfast to Islam, even when Pharaoh reached her youngest child, a baby boy still breast feeding, but she felt pity for him. At that, Allah enabled this child to speak. He said to his mother, "O Mother, be patient. The torture of the Hereafter is far more severe than the torture of this life, and do not be reluctant, because you are right." At this the woman requested Pharaoh collect her bones and the bones of her children and bury them in the same grave. Pharaoh promised her that, then dropped her into that boiling water. She died as a martyr. The good odour the Prophet smelled coming from her grave is an indication of her high status.

4. During his trip, the Prophet (P. B. B. U. H.) saw people who were planting and reaping in two days. Jibril (a.s.) told the Prophet, "These were the people who fight for the sake of Allah (mujahidun)."

5. The Prophet (P. B. B. U. H.) also saw people whose lips and tongues were clipped with scissors made of fire. Jibril (a.s.) told the Prophet, "These are the speakers of sedition (fitna) who call people to misguidance. "

6. He also saw a bull which exited a very small outlet, then was trying in vain to return through that small outlet. Jibril (a.s.) told the

Prophet (P. B. B. U. H.), "This is the example of the bad word-once spoken, it cannot be returned."

7. The Prophet (P. B. B. U. H.) saw people grazing like animals, with very little clothing on their private parts. Jibril (a.s.) told the Prophet (P. B. B. U. H.), "These are the ones who refused to pay zakat."

8. The Prophet (P. B. B. U. H.) saw angels smashing some people's heads with rocks. These heads would return to the shape they had been, and then the angels would smash their heads again-and so on. Jibril (a.s.) told the Prophet (P. B. B. U. H.), "These are the ones whose heads felt too heavy to perform prayer–the ones who used to sleep without praying."

9. On his journey the Prophet (P. B. B. U. H.) saw people who were competing to eat some rotten meat-ignoring meat that was sliced and unspoiled. Jibril (a.s.) told the Prophet, "These are people from your nation who leave out that which is permissible (halal), and consume that which is forbidden (haram). "This reference was to the fornicators, that is, the ones who left out the permissible (marriage) and committed sins (fornication) .

10. Also, the Prophet (P. B. B. U. H.) saw people who were drinking from the fluid coming from the bodies of the fornicators, (water mixed with blood). Jibril (a.s.) indicated to the Prophet these were the ones who were drinking the alcohol which is prohibited in this world.

11. The Prophet (P. B. B. U. H.) saw people scratching their faces and chests with brass finger nails. Jibril (a.s.) said, "These are the examples of those who commit gossip (gheebah)."

*[Tafsir Qurtubi]

**[Tafsir Ibn Kathir]

*Originally, Iblees was a believer and lived with the angels in Paradise . When Allah ordered the angels to prostrate (sujud) to Prophet Adam (a.s.), Iblees was ordered to prostrate to him as well. The angels prostrated to Adam in obedience to Allah, because angels do not disobey Allah. However, Iblis did not obey, and he objected to the order of Allah. He said, "You created me out of fire, and You created him out of clay. How do You order me to prostrate to him?" So this objection by Iblees to the order of Allah was the first blasphemy he committed.

Appendix D
Supremacy of Muhammad[111]

(Authors' comment: The following is response to the question whereby the questioner sees that the Jews have a legitimate stake in Jerusalem, but whereby the responder, a top Islamic authority vehemently and "systematically" builds the Islamic argument that even if the Jews had some presence in the holy land, they had forfeited any and all rights because of their "unbelief" And hence, Jerusalem should be 100% an Islamic property forever).

Question: I hear some people saying that intercession belongs only to Allaah and can only be asked of Him, while others say that Allaah has given the power of intercession to His Prophet (peace and blessings of Allaah be upon him) and to His righteous close friends (awliyaa') so that we may ask them to intercede for us. What is the correct view, and can you quote shar'i evidence to support it?

Response by top Islamic scholar on the Types of intercession (shafaa'ah)

Praise be to Allaah.

Intercession means mediating for someone else to gain some benefit or ward off some harm.

It is of two types:

The first type: intercession that will take place in the Hereafter, on the Day of Resurrection.

The second type: intercession concerning matters of this world.

---

[111] http://islamqa.com/en/ref/26259

With regard to the intercession that will take place in the Hereafter, it is of two types:

The first type: exclusive intercession, which will be granted only to the Messenger (peace and blessings of Allaah be upon him), and no one else in creation will have a share in that with him. This is of various kinds:

1. The greater intercession. This is the station of praise and glory (al-maqaam al-mahmood) which Allaah has promised to him, when He said (interpretation of the meaning):

    "And in some parts of the night (also) offer the Salaat (prayer) with it (i.e. recite the Qur'aan in the prayer) as an additional prayer (Tahajjud optional prayer Nawaafil) for you (O Muhammad). It may be that your Lord will raise you to Maqaam Mahmood (a station of praise and glory, i.e., the honour of intercession on the Day of Resurrection)" [al-Isra' 17:79]

    What this intercession means is that he will intercede for all of mankind when Allaah delays the Reckoning and they have waited for so long in the place of gathering on the Day of Resurrection. Their distress and anxiety will reach a point where they can no longer bear it, and they will say, "Who will intercede for us with our Lord so that He will pass judgement amongst His slaves?" and they will wish to leave that place. So the people will come to the Prophets, each of whom will say, "I am not able for it," until when they come to our Prophet (peace and blessings of Allaah be upon him), he will say, "I am able for it, I am able for it." So he will intercede for them, that judgement may be passed. This is the greater intercession, and it is one of the things that belong exclusively to the Prophet (peace and blessings of Allaah be upon him).

    There are many ahaadeeth[112] which speak of this intercession, in al-Saheehayn and elsewhere, such as the hadeeth narrated by al-Bukhaari in his Saheeh (1748) from Ibn 'Umar (may Allaah be

---

[112] "ahaadeeth" is the plural of Hadith in Arabic "hadeeth is another spelling of Hadith" (Author's note).

pleased with him): "The people will fall on their knees on the Day of Resurrection, each nation following its Prophet, saying, 'O So and so, intercede!' until intercession is granted to the Prophet (peace and blessings of Allaah be upon him). On that Day Allaah will resurrect him to a station of praise and glory."

2. Intercession for the people of Paradise to enter Paradise.

It was narrated that Anas ibn Maalik said: "The Messenger of Allaah (peace and blessings of Allaah be upon him) said: 'I will come to the gate of Paradise on the Day of Resurrection and will ask for it to be opened. The gatekeeper will say, "Who are you?" I will say, "Muhammad." He will say, "I was commanded not to open it for anyone before you."'" (Narrated by Muslim, 333).

According to another report narrated by Muslim (332), "I will be the first one to intercede concerning Paradise."

3. The intercession of the Messenger (peace and blessings of Allaah be upon him) for his uncle Abu Taalib:

It was narrated from Abu Sa'eed al-Khudri (may Allaah be pleased with him) that mention was made of his uncle Abu Taalib in the presence of the Messenger of Allaah (peace and blessings of Allaah be upon him). He said, "Perhaps my intercession will benefit him on the Day of Resurrection, and he will be placed in a shallow part of the Fire which will come up to his ankles and cause his brains to boil." (Narrated by al-Bukhaari, 1408; Muslim, 360).

4. His intercession so that some people of his ummah will enter Paradise without being brought to account.

This kind of intercession was mentioned by some of the scholars, who quoted as evidence the lengthy hadeeth of Abu Hurayrah concerning intercession, in which it says: "Then it will be said, 'O Muhammad, raise you head; ask, it will be given to you; intercede, your intercession will be accepted.' So I will raise my head and say, 'My ummah, O Lord; my ummah, O Lord; my ummah, O Lord.' It will be said, 'Admit those among your ummah who are not to be brought to account through the right-hand gate of Paradise. They will share the other gates with the people of other nations.'" (Narrated by al-Bukhaari, 4343; Muslim, 287).

The second type: general intercession. This will be granted to the Messenger (peace and blessings of Allaah be upon him) and others — angels, Prophets and righteous people — will share in it as Allaah wills. This is of various kinds:

1. Intercession for some people who have entered Hell, that they might be brought forth from it. There is a great deal of evidence for this, for example:

   The marfoo' hadeeth of Abu Sa'eed al-Khudri (may Allaah be pleased with him) in Saheeh Muslim (269): "By the One in Whose hand is my soul, none of you can be more insistent in asking Allaah to restore his rights against his opponent than the believers who will ask Allaah, on the Day of Resurrection, (to grant them the power of intercession) for their brothers who are in the Fire. They will say, 'Our Lord, they used to fast with us and pray and perform Hajj.' It will be said to them, 'Bring out those whom you recognize, so the Fire will be forbidden to burn them.' So they will bring out many people…And Allaah will say: 'The angels have interceded, and the Prophets have interceded, and the believers have interceded. There is none left but the Most Merciful of those who show mercy.' Then He will seize a handful of the Fire and bring forth from it people who never did anything good."

2. Intercession for people who deserve Hell, that they may not enter it. This may be indicated by the words of the Prophet (peace and blessings of Allaah be upon him): "There is no Muslim who dies and forty men who associate nothing with Allaah pray the funeral prayer for him, but Allaah will accept their intercession for him." (Narrated by Muslim, 1577). For this intercession happens before the deceased enters Hell, and Allaah will accept their intercession concerning that.

3. Intercession for some of the believers who deserve Paradise, that they may be raised in status in Paradise. For example, Muslim (may Allaah have mercy on him) narrated (1528) that the Prophet (peace and blessings of Allaah be upon him) prayed for Abu Salamah and said: "O Allaah, forgive Abu Salamah and raise his status among those who are guided, and take good care of his family that he has left behind. Forgive us and him, O Lord of the Worlds, make his grave spacious for him and illuminate it for him."

Conditions of this intercession:

The evidence indicates that intercession in the Hereafter will only happen if the following conditions are met:

1) Allaah must approve of the one for whom intercession is made, because Allaah says (interpretation of the meaning): "and they cannot intercede except for him with whom He is pleased" [al-Anbiya' 21:28]

   This implies that the one for whom intercession is made must be a believer in Tawheed, because Allaah is not pleased with the mushrikeen. In Saheeh al-Bukhaari (97) it is narrated from Abu Hurayrah (may Allaah be pleased with him) that he said: "It was said, 'O Messenger of Allaah, who will be the most blessed of people by your intercession of the Day of Resurrection?' The Messenger of Allaah (peace and blessings of Allaah be upon him) said: "I thought, O Abu Hurayrah, that no one would ask me about this hadeeth before you, because I have seen how keen you are to learn hadeeth. The people who will be most blessed by my intercession on the Day of Resurrection are those who say Laa ilaaha ill-Allaah sincerely from the heart.'"

2) Allaah must give permission to the intercessor to intercede, because Allaah says (interpretation of the meaning):"Who is he that can intercede with Him except with His Permission?" [al-Baqarah 2:255]

3) Allaah must approve of the intercessor, because Allaah says (interpretation of the meaning): "…whose intercession will avail noth-

ing except after Allaah has given leave for whom He wills and is pleased with" [al-Najm 53:26]

And the Messenger (peace and blessings of Allaah be upon him) has stated that those who curse much will not be intercessors on the Day of Resurrection, as Muslim narrated in his Saheeh (4703) that Abu'l-Darda' (may Allaah be pleased with him) said: "I heard the Messenger of Allaah (peace and blessings of Allaah be upon him) say, 'Those who curse much will not be witnesses or intercessors on the Day of Resurrection.'"

The second type of intercession is that which has to do with matters of this world. This is of two types:

1. That which is within a person's ability to do something. This is permissible, subject to two conditions:

   1) That it should have to do with a permissible thing. It is not correct to intercede concerning something that will result in the loss of people's rights or in wrong being done to them. It is also not correct to intercede concerning something that is haraam, such as those who intercede concerning those who deserve the hadd punishment, asking that it not be carried out on them. Allaah says (interpretation of the meaning):

      "Help you one another in Al-Birr and At-Taqwa (virtue, righteousness and piety); but do not help one another in sin and transgression" [al-Maa'idah 5:2]

According to a hadeeth narrated by 'Aa'ishah (may Allaah be pleased with her), Quraysh were concerned about a Makhzoomi woman who had stolen, and they said, "Who will speak to the Messenger of Allaah (peace and blessings of Allaah be upon him) concerning her? Who better than Usaamah, the beloved of the Messenger of Allaah (peace and blessings of Allaah be upon him)?" So Usaamah spoke to him, and the Messenger of Allaah (peace and blessings of Allaah be upon him) said, "Are you interceding concerning one of the hadd punishments prescribed by Allaah?" Then he stood up and addressed the people, and said, "O people, those who came before you were only destroyed because if one of their nobles stole they would let him off but if one of the weak stole they would carry out the punishment on him. By Allaah, if Faatimah the daughter of Muhammad were to steal, I would cut off her hand." (Narrated by al-Bukhaari, 3261; Muslim, 3196).

In Saheeh al-Bukhaari (5568) and Saheeh Muslim (4761) it is narrated that Abu Moosa (may Allaah be pleased with him) said that if someone came with a need to the Messenger of Allaah (peace and blessings of Allaah be upon him), he would turn to those who were sitting with him and say, "Intercede, and you will be rewarded, and Allaah will decree what He wills through the lips of His Messenger."

2) In his heart, the person must depend on Allaah alone to realize his aim and ward off what is disliked. He should know that this intercessor is no more than a means which Allaah has permitted to us, and that benefit and harm are in the hand of Allaah alone. This meaning is expressed clearly in the Book of Allaah and the Sunnah of His Messenger (peace and blessings of Allaah be upon him).

If either of these two conditions is not met, then the intercession is not allowed.

2. That which is not within a person's ability to do something, such as seeking intercession from the dead and occupants of graves, or from a living person who is absent, believing that he is able to hear and meet one's need. This is the kind of intercession that constitutes shirk, which is clearly forbidden in many verses of the Qur'aan and ahaadeeth from the Prophet (peace and blessings of Allaah be upon him), because it ascribes to them attributes which belong only to the Creator, for He is the Ever-living Who never dies.

Their specious argument is that the awliya' ("saints") and Sayyids intercede for their relatives and for those who call on them and take them as friends and love them, and because of that they ask them for intercession. This is exactly what Allaah described the early mushrikeen as doing, when they said,

"These are our intercessors with Allaah"

[Yoonus 10:18 – interpretation of the meaning]

- referring to those whom they worshipped among the angels, righteous people and others, and meaning that they would intercede for them with Allaah. In the same way, the contemporary mushrikoon say "the awliya' ('saints') intercede for us; we cannot ask of Allaah (directly) so we ask them and they ask of Allaah." And they say that the Prophet (peace and blessings of Allaah be upon him) and all the Prophets and righteous people were given the power of intercession, and we call upon them and say, intercede for us as Allaah has given you the power of intercession. They give the example of kings in this world, and say that the kings of this world can only be approached through intercession; if you need something, you go to their friends and those who are close to them, their ministers, gatekeepers, servants, etc., to intercede for you so that the king can deal with your matter; so we reach Allaah by approaching and asking His awliyaa' and the Sayyids who are close to Him. By doing this they fall into the same shirk as those who came before them, and they compare the Creator to His creation.

Allaah tells us of a righteous man in Soorat Ya-Seen, who said (interpretation of the meaning):

"'Shall I take besides Him aalihah (gods)? If the Most Gracious (Allaah) intends me any harm, their intercession will be of no use for me whatsoever" [Ya-Seen 36:23]

And Allaah tells us that the kuffaar will confess it themselves:

"They will say: 'We were not of those who used to offer the Salaah (prayers),

Nor we used to feed Al-Miskeen (the poor);

And we used to talk falsehood (all that which Allaah hated) with vain talkers.

And we used to belie the Day of Recompense, Until there came to us (the death) that is certain', So no intercession of intercessors will be of any use to them"

[al-Muddaththir 74:43-48 — interpretation of the meaning]

The Prophet (peace and blessings of Allaah be upon him), even though he will be given the power of intercession on the Day of Resurrection, will not be able to use it until after Allaah has given him permission and has approved of the one for whom intercession is to be made.

Hence he (peace and blessings of Allaah be upon him) did not let his ummah ask him to intercede for them in this world, and that was not narrated from any one of his Sahaabah (may Allaah be pleased with them). If that had been a good thing, he would have conveyed it to his ummah and called them to do it, and his Companions who were keen to do good would have hastened to do it. Thus we know that seeking intercession from him now (in this world) is a great wrong, because it involves calling upon someone other than Allaah and doing something which is an obstacle to intercession, for intercession is available only to those who sincerely believe in Allaah alone (Tawheed).

The people in the place of standing (on the Day of Resurrection) will only ask the Prophet (peace and blessings of Allaah be upon him) to intercede for them so that judgement will be passed, because he will be there with them and because he will be able to turn to his Lord and ask Him. This is like asking a person who is alive and present to do make du'aa' for one, which is something that he is able to do.

Hence it is not narrated that any of the people in the place of standing will ask him (peace and blessings of Allaah be upon him) to intercede for them that their sins might be forgiven.

Those who ask him for intercession now, based on the fact that it will be permissible to ask him for that in the Hereafter, if their claims were justified, would have to limit what they say to, "O Messenger of Allaah, intercede for us that judgement may be passed"! But they do something other than that. They do not limit it to a request for intercession, rather they ask the Prophet (peace and blessings of Allaah be upon him) — and others – to relieve their distress and send down mercy; they turn to him at times of calamity; they pray to him on land and sea, at times of ease and times of difficulty, ignoring the words of Allaah (interpretation of the meaning):

"Is not He (better than your gods) Who responds to the distressed one, when he calls on Him, and Who removes the evil, and makes you inheritors of the earth, generations after generations?"[al-Naml 27:62]

From the above it is clear to every fair-minded person that the correct kind of intercession is intercession that depends on the permission and approval of Allaah, because all intercession belongs to Him. That also includes asking for intercession from living people who are able to do that concerning worldly matters, for which Allaah has granted permission. It should be pointed out here that this kind of intercession is permitted because Allaah has given permission for it, since it involves no kind of emotional attachment to the person, rather the point is that it is a means, like all other means which Islam permits us to use. The kind of intercession which is forbidden is asking someone other than Allaah to do something that no one is able to do except Allaah, because intercession belongs to no one besides Allaah, and no one can do it unless Allaah grants him leave and approves of him. So whoever seeks intercession from anyone else has transgressed upon the exclusive preserve of Allaah and has wronged himself, and has exposed himself to being deprived of the intercession of the Prophet (peace and blessings of Allaah be upon him) on the Day of Resurrection. We ask Allaah to keep us safe and sound, and we ask Him to cause our Prophet (peace and blessings of Allaah be upon him) to intercede for us...Ameen.

For more information see al-Shafaa'ah 'inda Ahl al-Sunnah wa'l-Jamaa'ah by Shaykh Naasir al-Juday'; al-Qawl al-Mufeed by Shaykh Muhammad ibn 'Uthaymeen, 1/423; A'laam al-Sunnah al-Manshoorah, 144.

Sheikh Muhammed Salih Al-Munajjid

Appendix e
Another Commentary on the Supremacy of Muhammad[113]

(Authors' note: The following is an Islamic scholarly opinion that considers the significance of Muhammad's allegation that he had led all the prophets in prayer during his night journey to Jerusalem showing his characteristics as supreme over all prophets, hence mankind, and the "leader of the sons of Adam on the Day of Resurrection and the first for whom the grave will be opened and the first to intercede and the first whose intercession will be accepted.")

Q uestion: What is the reason why the Prophet Muhammad (peace and blessings of Allaah be upon him) led the other prophets in prayer on the night of the Isra'? What does this indicate?

Response: The reason why the Prophet (peace and blessings of Allaah be upon him) led the other Prophets in prayer during the Isra' (Night Journey)

Praise be to Allaah.

The reason why the Prophet (peace and blessings of Allaah be upon him) was made to go forward to lead the other Prophets in prayer in al-Masjid al-Aqsa, which is the home of the Prophets from Ibraaheem al-Khaleel (peace be upon him) is that our Prophet Muhammad (peace and blessings of Allaah be upon him) is the greatest leader, as was stated by al-Haafiz ibn Katheer (may Allaah have mercy on him) at the beginning of

---

[113] http://islamqa.com/en/ref/46917/night%20journey (Islam Q&A)

his commentary on Soorat al-Isra'. He also said, when discussing how the Prophet (peace and blessings of Allaah be upon him) led the other Prophets in prayer: "Then his honourable status and superiority to them was manifested when he was made to go forward to lead them in prayer, when Jibreel (peace be upon him) indicated to him that he should do so."

Undoubtedly our Prophet (peace and blessings of Allaah be upon him) is the foremost among the Prophets. He (peace and blessings of Allaah be upon him) said: "I will be the leader of the sons of Adam on the Day of Resurrection and the first for whom the grave will be opened and the first to intercede and the first whose intercession will be accepted."

Narrated by Al-Muslim, 2278.

One of the scholars suggested another reason why he (peace and blessings of Allaah be upon him) was made to go forward to lead the Prophets in prayer. He said: The Prophet's words, "I led them (in prayer)" indicate — and Allaah knows best — that this ummah took over the position of leading mankind.

And Allaah knows best.

Appendix F
Muhammad above All Prophets[114]

(Authors' note: In Chapter 4 we explain how the original covenant imposed on mankind by Allah has a second component whereby all the prophets are required to accept Muhammad and his message, thus making them all "Muslims.")

Question: I help teach a group of girls about Islam once a week. This past week, one of the girls asked me the following question, to which, I was not able to reply and I told her that I would look it up or ask someone. The question was: Are all the prophets considered equal? If so, then why is it that the there is a prophet on each level of heaven, with Prophet Muhammad (SAAS) in the highest (seventh heaven)?

Response by top Islamic authority Sheikh Muhammed Salih Al-Munajjid: Are the Prophets equal?

Praise be to Allaah.

All people were created by Allaah and are His slaves; His is the power and command from eternity to eternity. The wisdom of Allaah decreed that He should select some of His angels and prefer them over others, such as Jibreel, Mika'eel, Israafeel, Maalik, Radwaan et al., who have a higher status than others. And His wisdom and justice decreed that He should select some of the children of Adam and prefer some of them over others,

---

[114] http://islamqa.com/en/ref/7459/bayt%20al%20maqdis

so that they have a higher status and better position. As Allaah says (interpretation of the meaning):

"Allaah chooses Messengers from angels and from men. Verily, Allaah is All-Hearer, All-Seer" [al-Hajj 22:75]

"Those Messengers! We preferred some of them to others; to some of them Allaah spoke (directly); others He raised to degrees (of honour)" [al-Baqarah 2:253]

Allaah tells us that He chose and selected these Messengers from among mankind. After mentioning some of the Prophets and Messengers, He says (interpretation of the meaning):

"And also some of their fathers and their progeny and their brethren, We chose them, and We guided them to the Straight Path" [al-An'aam 6:87].

And Allaah says (interpretation of the meaning):

"And Allaah has preferred some of you above others in wealth and properties" [al-Nahl 16:71].

His wisdom decreed that Adam (peace be upon him) should be the father of mankind, and His wisdom, mercy and justice decreed that from among Adam's progeny He should select an elite of Messengers and Prophets – may peace and blessings be upon them and upon our Prophet. Among those whom He chose and preferred over others were the Messengers of strong will [Uloo'l-'Azm, see al-Ahqaaf 46:35], namely, Muhammad, Ibraaheem, Nooh, Moosa and 'Eesaa ibn Maryam, may the best of blessings and peace be upon them. And He chose and favoured above them all their leader, the final Messenger, our Prophet Muhammad ibn 'Abd-Allaah (peace and blessings of Allaah be upon him). He is indeed the leader of the sons of Adam, with no boast. He will carry the banner and will be granted the power of intercession [on the Day of Resurrection]. He is the one who will attain al-maqaam al-mahmood (the Praised Position) in Paradise, which will be given to one person only, and that person will be our Prophet (peace and blessings of Allaah be upon him). Hence Allaah took the covenant and pledge from all the Prophets that if Muhammad (peace and blessings of Allaah be upon him) was sent during the lifetime of any one of them, they would be obliged to follow him (peace and blessings of Allaah be upon him), to leave behind what they had brought and follow what our Prophet (peace and blessings of Allaah be upon him) brought. As Allaah says (interpretation of the meaning):

"And (remember) when Allaah took the Covenant of the Prophets, saying: 'Take whatever I gave you from the Book and Hikmah (understanding of the Laws of Allaah), and afterwards there will come to you a Messenger (Muhammad) confirming what is with you; you must, then, believe in him and help him.' Allaah said: 'Do you agree (to it) and will you take up My Covenant (which I conclude with you)?' They said: 'We agree.' He said: 'Then bear witness; and I am with you among the witnesses (for this).' Then whoever turns away after this, they are the Faasiqoon (rebellious: those who turn away from Allaah's obedience)" [Aal-Imraan 3:81-82]

The Prophet (peace and blessings of Allaah be upon him) said to 'Umar ibn al-Khattaab (may Allaah be pleased with him): "By Allaah, if my brother Moosa were alive, he would have no choice but to follow me."

And when the Messiah 'Eesaa ibn Maryam (peace be upon him) comes down at the end of time, he will come to rule in accordance with the sharee'ah of Muhammad (peace and blessings of Allaah be upon him), and he will follow him (peace and blessings of Allaah be upon him).

All of the above refers to their status before Allaah. With regard to their religion, it is one religion, for they all called people to believe in One God, Allaah (Tawheed) and to devote worship sincerely to Him Alone. With regard to laws, each of them had his own law which was for his people alone. Allaah says (interpretation of the meaning):

"To each among you, We have prescribed a law and a clear way" [al-Maa'idah 5:48]. But the way (sharee'ah) of our Prophet Muhammad (peace and blessings of Allaah be upon him) is the most perfect, the best, the most complete and the most beloved to Allaah; it abrogates all laws that came before it. Undoubtedly the Prophets differ in status, and they are at varying levels. The best of them, as stated above, are the five Messengers of strong will (Uloo'l-'Azm), and the best of them all is the Seal of the Prophets, Muhammad (peace and blessings of Allaah be upon him).

With regard to the saheeh ahaadeeth, "Do not prefer me over Yoonus ibn Mattaa" and "By the One Who chose Moosa over all of creation" — these all indicate the immense humility of the Prophet (peace and blessings of Allaah be upon him) when speaking of his brothers the Messengers. But he is undoubtedly the best of them all, for he led them in prayer in Bayt al-Maqdis (Jerusalem) on the night of the Israa'. He will be the leader of the sons of Adam on the Day of Resurrection, and he is the only one among all the Messengers who will be granted the power of intercession on that Day. He (peace and blessings of Allaah be upon him) is the one who said: "From among the sons of Adam, Allaah chose Quraysh; from among Quraysh He chose Kinaanah; from among Kinaanah He chose Bani Haashim; and from among Bani Haashim He chose me." He (peace and blessings of Allaah be upon him) is the Chosen One (al-Mustafaa) from among all of mankind.

And Allaah knows best.

Islam Q&A
Sheikh Muhammed Salih Al-Munajjid

Appendix G
Importance of the Qibla, Direction of Prayer

(Authors' note: Although the Qibla seems to the uninitiated observer as an innocuous issue in relation to the theme of this book, we have included this Islamic scholarly discussion of it to point out the background associated with the changing of the Qibla from Jerusalem to Mecca. The reader may be puzzled, why Mecca after Jerusalem? The response should provide relevant background information on how systematically Muhammad severed his relationship with the Jews while appropriating their spiritual and historical capital to Islam.)

Q uestion: What should one who is informed about the correct direction of the qiblah during a prayer?

Response by Sheikh Muhammed Salih Al-Munajjid: Information about correct direction of qiblah during prayer

If there is a congregation praying, and during their prayer they are informed about the right direction of qiblah, they should all turn towards the correct direction. The same is also true for someone praying individually. Whatever part of their prayer has been performed (before changing direction) will be correct. The evidence for this a narration by Imam Muslim from Anas (may Allah be please with him), that:

While the Prophet (peace be upon him) was praying towards Bayt-al-Maqdis (Jerusalem), the verse was revealed to him (translation of meaning):

Verily! We have seen the turning of your face towards the heaven. Surely, We shall turn you to a qiblah that shall please you, so turn your face in the direction of Al-Masjid Al-Haram.

(Al-Baqarah, 2:144).

A man from Bani Salamah was passing by and found them (i.e., the people of Bani Salamah) in the state of ruku' in the Fajr prayer in the second rak'ah. He shouted to them: Indeed the qiblah has been changed. So, turn to the qiblah as they (i.e., the Prophet and his Companions) have.

(Sahih Musim, No. 527)

If some of the people were informed and the others were not, then the one to whom it was made clear should turn to the direction he believes to be the correct direction of qiblah. Now if all of these people (who were informed or not) were originally praying together in the same direction, and some of them turned towards right and some towards left, it is correct for some to follow others. But the scholars have a difference of opinion about some people following others in the situation where there was complete disagreement (among the praying people) about the direction of the qiblah. If there was someone among them who was completely ignorant about the direction, he should follow the one who is more aware amongst them of the direction of the qiblah. For the one who was uninformed about the direction of the qiblah, must ask someone if he can, or else he should make ijtihad (make a judgment based on the best of his ability with the information available) if he is able to, otherwise he must follow someone who is reliable. If he cannot find one, then he should do his best in obedience to Allah and complete his prayer, and his prayer is correct. This sometimes happens to a number of those who travel to the lands of disbelievers and find no Muslim around them to inform them of the correct direction of qiblah.

If one was capable of finding out the direction of the qiblah, but was neglectful and prayed without making all possible efforts, he should repeat his prayer because he was careless.

1 Al-Mughni, 1/473.
2 Al-Mughni, 1/490.

Islam Q&A
Sheikh Muhammed Salih Al-Munajjid

Appendix h
Fatwa Regarding the Qibla[115]

(Authors' note: Taking off from the previous appendix on the Qibla, we provide herein a complete "Fatwa" by a top committee of senior Islamic scholars in Saudi Arabia, affirming Islam's superiority over Jews and Christians. Note that aside from the strong denigration of the Jews, Christians have been accorded another form of denigration as they pray "toward the East!" Amazingly, the Fatwa scholars quote some New Testament verses to support their case. Of course, one is puzzled by their firm belief that Christians pray toward the East, let alone their assumption that the Christian prayer is ritual, like the Islamic prayer.)

Question: Is the qiblah of the Muslims when they pray always towards the East?

Response by top Fatwa Committee in Saudi Arabia

Please why do Muslims face the east in prayers. Please your answer with references.

Praise be to Allaah.

Firstly:

The Muslims turn to face the Ka'bah when they pray, in response to the command of Allaah, This is the qiblah (direction of prayer) of their father Ibraaheem (peace be upon him).

There is great wisdom in this command to turn towards the Ka'bah when praying.

---

[115] http://islamqa.com/en/ref/115825/bayt%20al%20maqdis

The scholars of the Standing Committee for issuing Fatwas were asked: What is the wisdom behind the Muslims taking the Ka'bah as their qiblah or direction of prayer?

They replied:

It is no secret that the Muslim is required to do whatever he can of the things that are enjoined, and to refrain from all the haraam things that are forbidden, whether or not he understands the wisdom behind the prohibition, whilst believing that Allaah does not command His slaves to do anything but that which is in their best interests, and He does not forbid them to do anything but that which is harmful to them. His laws are all for a reason which is known to Him, and He makes apparent whatever He wills of it, so that the believer will increase in faith thereby. And He conceals whatever He wills thereof, so as to increase the believer in submission to the command of Allaah out of faith.

The Muslims take the Ka'bah as their direction of prayer in response to the command of Allaah in the verse where He says (interpretation of the meaning):

"Verily, We have seen the turning of your (Muhammad's) face towards the heaven. Surely, We shall turn you to a Qiblah (prayer direction) that shall please you, so turn your face in the direction of Al-Masjid Al-Haraam (at Makkah). And wheresoever you people are, turn your faces (in prayer) in that direction"

[al-Baqraah 2:144]

Perhaps one of the reasons why Allaah commanded them to do that is that it was the qiblah of their father Ibraaheem (peace be upon him). It is also narrated concerning the reason for revelation of this verse that our Prophet (peace and blessings of Allaah be upon him) wanted to be commanded to turn to face the Ka'bah when praying instead of turning towards Bayt al-Maqdis (Jerusalem), and Allaah commanded him to do that.

It may also have been to put an end to the Jews' argument that he was facing the same direction of prayer as they did.

And it may have been for other reasons. Allaah knows best. End quote.

Shaykh 'Abd al-'Azeez ibn Baaz, Shaykh 'Abd al-Razzaaq 'Afeefi, Shaykh 'Abd-Allaah ibn Ghadyaan, Shaykh 'Abd-Allaah ibn Qa'ood.

Fataawa al-Lajnah al-Daa'imah (6/311, 312)

For more information please see the answer to question no. 1953.

Secondly:

It is not correct to say that the Muslims face east when praying, rather for some Muslims the Ka'bah may be in the east, or it may be in the west or the north or the south. That varies according to the geographical position of a country in relation to Makkah al-Mukarramah.

As for those whose direction of prayer is always to the east, they are some groups of Christians, not Muslims!

Allaah says (interpretation of the meaning):

"And even if you were to bring to the people of the Scripture (Jews and Christians) all the Ayaat (proofs, evidences, verses, lessons, signs, revelations, etc.), they would not follow your Qiblah (prayer direction), nor are you going to follow their Qiblah (prayer direction). And they will not follow each other's Qiblah (prayer direction). Verily, if you follow their desires after that which you have received of knowledge (from Allaah), then indeed you will be one of the Zaalimoon (polytheists, wrongdoers)"

[al-Baqarah 2:145]

Imam al-Tabari (may Allaah have mercy on him) said:

With regard to the words "nor are you going to follow their Qiblah (prayer direction)", He is saying: You have no way, O Muhammad, of following their direction of prayer, because the Jews turn to face Jerusalem when they pray, and the Christians face towards the east. So how can you follow their direction of prayer when they differ from one another? So stick to the qiblah which you have been commanded to turn towards, and ignore what the Jews and Christians say when they call you to turn towards their qiblah.

Tafseer al-Tabari (3/185).

Ibn Qudaamah (may Allaah have mercy on him) said in al-Mughni (1/429) that the Christians turned towards the East, and the Christians' turning towards the east is one aspect of the way in which they have distorted their religion and gone against the Messiah and the Gospel.

Shaykh Saalih ibn al-Husayn al-Ja'fari al-Haashimi said:

Another issue is that the Christians pray towards the east, where the sun rises, and they take this as their direction of prayer. The Messiah (peace be upon him) throughout his stay on earth, prayed towards Bayt al-Maqdis or Jerusalem, which was the qiblah of Moosa ibn 'Imraan and the Prophets. He said:

"Do not think that I have come to abolish the Law or the Prophets; I have not come to abolish them but to fulfill them.

18 I tell you the truth, until heaven and earth disappear, not the smallest letter, not the least stroke of a pen, will by any means disappear from the Law until everything is accomplished"

[Matthew 5:17-18]

But the Christians went against the Messiah and the Prophets, and they gave as their excuse for turning to face towards the east the notion that this is the direction facing which their Lord was crucified and their God was killed.

It may be said to them:

O fools! If you had any understanding you would hate the direction of the east, and despise it, and regard it as inauspicious, and you would refuse it in ordinary matters, let alone matters of worship, because it is not the direction towards which the Messiah prayed and the Gospels do not testify to that. None of the Prophets prayed facing it at all. Moreover it is the direction from which you were destroyed and scattered and divided into groups. So the fact that you venerate this direction which is the worst of directions for you is something which makes a laughing-stock of you and brings scorn upon you. It would have been better for you not to turn away from the direction of Jerusalem because the Gospel says that the Samaritan woman said to the Messiah:

" 'Sir…our fathers worshiped on this mountain, but you Jews claim that the place where we must worship is in Jerusalem.'

21 Jesus declared, 'Believe me, woman,…you Samaritans worship what you do not know; we worship what we do know'"

[John 4:19-21]

Here the Messiah is testifying that God has no direction which is to be faced in prayer except Bayt al-Maqdis, which is Jerusalem. Do you know better than the Messiah what God has enjoined? Verily we belong to God and unto Him is our return; we mourn the loss of your reason, which lead to your doom. End quote.

Takhjeel man harrafa al-Tawraat wa'l-Injeel (2/591, 592)

Thus it is clear that the questioner is mistaken in thinking that the Muslims always face towards the east when they pray, and it is clear that this is the religious practice of the Christians.

And Allaah knows best.

Islam Q&A

Appendix i

Relationship between the Al-Aqsa Mosque and Dome of the Rock[116]

(Authors' note: This Q&A from Islamic sources provides insight into how Muslims view the entire issue relating it to such assumptions that "King Solomon" built the Al-Aqsa Mosque, among other issues. Of course, this is a convenient assumption, as the Al-Aqsa Mosque had not been built when Muhammad went on his alleged night journey. The reader is advised to examine the details of this Islamic scholarly opinion and relate it to both Chapters 4 and 6).

Question: I have recently received an Email advising me of the status of the Masjid al Aqsa and differentiating it from the doom of the rock. Can you please clarify the situation and advise, if the Masjid e Aqsa is different from the Doom of the Rock, why do we see its picture representing Masjid e Aqsa at all Islamic places, and I (and many other muslims) were completely inaware of the difference?

Response by Islam Q&A on the topic of al-Masjid al-Aqsa and the Dome of the Rock

Praise be to Allaah.

Al-Masjid al-Aqsa (in Jerusalem) was the first of the two qiblahs, and is one of the three mosques to which people may travel for the purpose of

---

[116] http://islamqa.com/en/ref/20903/bayt%20al%20maqdis

worship. And it was said that it was built by Sulaymaan (peace be upon him), as stated in Sunan al-Nasaa'i (693) and classed as saheeh by al-Albaani in Saheeh al-Nasaa'i. And it was said that it existed before Sulaymaan (peace be upon him) and that Sulaymaan rebuilt it; this is based on the evidence narrated in al-Saheehayn from Abu Dharr (may Allaah be pleased with him) who said: "I said, 'O Messenger of Allaah, which mosque was built on earth first?' He said, 'Al-Masjid al-Haraam [in Makkah].' I said, 'Then which?' He said, 'Al-Masjid al-Aqsa.' I said, 'How much time was there between them?' He said, 'Forty years. So wherever you are when the time for prayer comes, pray, for that is the best thing to do.'"

Narrated by al-Bukhaari, 3366; Muslim, 520.

The Prophet (peace and blessings of Allaah be upon him) was taken on the Night Journey (isra') to Bayt al-Maqdis (Jerusalem), where he led the Prophets in prayer in this blessed mosque.

Allaah says (interpretation of the meaning):

"Glorified (and Exalted) be He (Allaah) [above all that (evil) they associate with Him]

Who took His slave (Muhammad) for a journey by night from Al-Masjid Al-Haraam (at Makkah) to Al-Masjid Al-Aqsaa (in Jerusalem), the neighbourhood whereof We have blessed, in order that We might show him (Muhammad) of Our Ayaat (proofs, evidences, lessons, signs, etc.). Verily, He is the All-Hearer, the All-Seer"

[al-Isra' 17:1]

The Dome of the Rock was built by the caliph 'Abd al-Malik ibn Marwaan in 72 AH.

It says in al-Mawsoo'ah al-Filasteeniyyah (4/203): "The name al-Masjid al-Aqsa was historically applied to the entire sanctuary (al-Haram al-Shareef) and the buildings in it, the most important of which is the Dome of the Rock which was built by 'Abd al-Malik ibn Marwaan in 72 AH/691 CE, which is regarded as one of the greatest Islamic historical buildings. But today the name is applied to the great mosque which is situated in the southern part of the sanctuary plateau."

It also says in al-Mawsoo'ah (3/23): "The Dome of the Rock is situated in the middle of the plateau of al-Masjid al-Aqsa, which is in the south-eastern part of the city of al-Quds (Jerusalem). It is a spacious rectangular plateau which measures 480 meters from north to south, and 300 meters from east to west. This plateau occupies approximately one-fifth of the area of the Old City of Jerusalem.

The mosque which is the place of prayer is not the Dome of the Rock, but because pictures of the Dome are so widespread, many Muslims think when they see it that this is the mosque. This is not in fact the case. The Mosque is situated in the southern portion of the plateau, and the Dome is built on the raised rock that is situated in the middle of the plateau.

We have already seen above that the name of the mosque was histori-cally applied to the whole plateau.

This is supported by the words of Shaykh al-Islam Ibn Taymiyah (may Allaah have mercy on him) in Majmoo'at al-Rasaa'il al-Kubra, 2/61: "Al-Masjid al-Aqsa is the name for the whole of the place of worship built by Sulaymaan (peace be upon him). Some people started to give the name of al-Aqsa to the prayer-place which was built by 'Umar ibn al-Khattaab in front of it. Praying in this prayer-place which 'Umar built for the Muslims is better than praying in the rest of the mosque, because when 'Umar conquered Jerusalem there was a huge garbage dump on the rock, since the Christians wanted to show their scorn for the place towards which the Jews used to pray. So 'Umar issued orders that the filth be removed and he said to Ka'b: 'Where do you think we should build a place of prayer for the Muslims?' He said, 'Behind the rock.' He said, 'O you son of a Jewish woman! Are influ-enced by your Jewish ideas! Rather I will build it in front of it.'

Hence when the imams of this ummah entered the mosque, they would go and pray in the prayer-place that was built by 'Umar. With regard to the Rock, neither 'Umar nor any of the Sahaabah prayed there, and there was no dome over it during the time of the Rightly-Guided Caliphs. It was open to the sky during the caliphate of 'Umar, 'Uthmaan, 'Ali, Mu'aawiyah, Yazeed and Marwaan...The scholars among the Sahaabah and those who followed them in truth did not venerate the rock because it was an abrogated qiblah... rather it was venerated by the Jews and some of the Christians."

'Umar denounced Ka'b al-Ahbaar and called him the son of a Jewish woman because Ka'b had been a Jewish scholar and rabbi, so when he suggested to 'Umar that he should build the mosque behind the rock, that was out of respect for the rock so that the Muslims would face it when praying, and veneration of the rock was part of the religion of the Jews, not the religion of the Muslims.

The Muslims' fondness for the picture of the Dome may be because of the beauty of this building, but this does not excuse them from the resulting mistake of not distinguishing between the Mosque and the buildings that surround it.

This may be one of the plots and tricks of the Jews, because of their veneration for the rock and their facing it in prayer. Or is may be in order to give importance to the Rock so that they can fulfil their desire to build the so-called Temple of Solomon on the ruins of al-Masjid al-Aqsa. This is by making the Muslims think that al-Masjid al-Aqsa is the Dome of the Rock, so that if the Jews start to destroy al-Masjid al-Aqsa and the Muslims denounce them for that, they will tell them, "Al-Masjid al-Aqsa is fine," and will show them a picture of the Dome of the Rock. Thus they will achieve their aims and be safe from the Muslims' criticism.

We ask Allaah to restore the Muslims' power and glory, and to cleanse al-Masjid al-Aqsa of the brothers of the monkeys and pigs, for Allaah has full power and control over His Affairs, but most of men know not (cf. Yoosuf 12:21).

And Allaah knows best.

Islam Q&A

Appendix J
Hebron Declared as Waqf Islamic Property Prior to Islamic Conquest of the Holy Lands[117]

(Authors' note: This very telling Islamic story demonstrates in part the rationale used to appropriate Hebron as an Islamic Waqf. The reader is advised to examine the details and the logic used to justify Islamic actions and to compare those with what is provided in both Chapters 4 and 6.)

Question: I heard that the Messenger of Allaah (peace and blessings of Allaah be upon him) gave al-Khaleel ("Hebron") in Palestine as a waqf to Banu Tameem, and that he wrote a document to that effect for them, and that 'Umar ibn al-Khattaab was one of those who witnessed it, and that they still live in al-Khaleel and are insisting on their rights to this waqf. Is this true, even though Palestine at that time was not under Muslim rule?

Response by Islam Q&A under the heading: Did the Prophet (peace and blessings of Allaah be upon him) give a waqf to Tameem al-Daari in Palestine?

Praise be to Allaah.

---

[117] http://islamqa.com/en/ref/52606/bayt%20al%20maqdis

It says in a number of reports that the Prophet (peace and blessings of Allaah be upon him) allocated Bayt Habroon or al-Khaleel to Tameem al-Daari.

Al-Haafiz Ibn Hajar (may Allaah have mercy on him) said:

Tameem ibn Aws ibn Khaarijah Abu Ruqayyah al-Daari moved to Greater Syria after the assassination of 'Uthmaan and he settled in Bayt al-Maqdis (Jerusalem). He converted in the year 9 AH.

Ya'qoob ibn Sufyaan said: He did not have any sons, but he had a daughter called Ruqayyah.

It was narrated from several sources that the Prophet (peace and blessings of Allaah be upon him) had allocated Bayt Habroon to him.

Tahdheeb al-Tahdheeb, 1/449

It says in Mu'jam al-Buldaan (2/212):

Habroon is the name of a town in which is located the grave of Ibraaheem al-Khaleel (peace be upon him) in Palestine. It is now known as al-Khaleel.

Tameem al-Daari came with his people to the Prophet (peace and blessings of Allaah be upon him) and asked him to allocate Habroon to him, and he responded and wrote a document for him, which says:

In the name of Allaah, the Most Gracious, the Most Merciful. This is what Muhammad the Messenger of Allaah has given to Tameem al-Daari and his companions. I give to you Bayt 'Aynoon, Habroon, al-Martoom and Bayt Ibraaheem and all that is in them; I give that to them and to their descendents for ever and ever. Whoever disputes with them concerning that is offending Allaah. Witnessed by Abu Bakr ibn Abi Quhaafah, 'Umar, 'Uthmaan and 'Ali ibn Abi Taalib. End quote.

At that time Palestine was not under Muslim control, rather it was ruled by the Byzantines. The Prophet (peace and blessings of Allaah be upon him) was allocating it for after Allaah enabled (the Muslims) to conquer it. So in this way the Prophet (peace and blessings of Allaah be upon him) was foretelling that it would be conquered.

When it was conquered during the reign of 'Umar, he fulfilled the promise of the Messenger of Allaah (peace and blessings of Allaah be upon him) and Tameem gave it as a waqf to his descendents. This was the first Islamic waqf ever in Palestine. Al-Maqdisi says in his book Ahsan al-Taqaaseem fi Ma'rifat al-Aqaaleem:

…There is a permanent guest-house with bakers, cooks and servants, which offers lentils in olive oil to every pilgrim or visitor who passes through the city of al-Khaleel. This hospitality and food is provided by the waqf of Tameem al-Daari (may Allaah be pleased with him).

Al-Qalqashandi said:

Al-Hamadaani said: The city of al-Khaleel is populated by Bani Tameem al-Daari (may Allaah be pleased with him), in whose possession is the document which was written by the Prophet (peace and blessings of Allaah be upon him) to Tameem and his brothers, allocating to them Bayt Habroon which is the town of al-Khaleel and some of its outskirts.

Subh al-A'sha, 1/47

And Allaah knows best.

Islam Q&A

Appendix k
Status of Al-Aqsa Mosque in Islam[118]

(Authors' note: Al-Aqsa Mosque is the third holiest Mosque in Islam, but what is its real relationship to the other two holy Mosques in Mecca and Medina? The reader is advised to carefully study the details of this Islamic scholarly opinion piece as it has bearing on the various hierarchies in Islamic thought, among other issues.)

Question: Is al-Masjid al-Aqsa considered to be a sanctuary (Haram) like the sanctuaries of Makkah and Madeenah?

Response by Islam Q&A under the heading: Is al-Masjid al-Aqsa considered to be a sanctuary?

Praise be to Allaah.

Firstly:

Al-Masjid al-Aqsa is superior to other mosques. The best of all mosques is al-Masjid al-Haraam (The Sacred Mosque in Makkah), then al-Masjid al-Nabawi (the Prophet's Mosque in Madeenah), then al-Masjid al-Aqsa.

These three mosques are the three for which it is prescribed to travel for the purpose of worship. The Prophet (peace and blessings of Allaah be upon him) said: "Do not travel (specifically) to any mosque except three: al-Masjid al-Haraam, Masjid al-Aqsa, and this mosque of mine."

---

[118] http://islamqa.com/en/ref/34751/bayt%20al%20maqdis

Narrated by al-Bukhaari, 1996.

One prayer in al-Masjid al-Aqsa is equivalent to two hundred and fifty prayers offered elsewhere.

It was narrated that Abu Dharr (may Allaah be pleased with him) said: We were discussing when we were with the Messenger of Allaah (peace and blessings of Allaah be upon him), which is better, the Mosque of the Messenger of Allaah (peace and blessings of Allaah be upon him) or Bayt al-Maqdis (Jerusalem). The Messenger of Allaah (peace and blessings of Allaah be upon him) said: "One prayer in my mosque is better than four prayers offered there (in Bayt al-Maqdis), and what a good place of prayer it is. Soon there will come a time when, if a man has a piece of land the size of a horse's rope from which he can see Bayt al-Maqdis, that will be better for him than the whole world." Narrated by al-Haakim, 4/509; he classed it as saheeh and al-Dhahabi and al-Albaani agreed with him, as it says in al-Silsilah al-Saheehah, at the end of the discussion on hadeeth no. 2902.

One prayer offered in the Prophet's Mosque is equivalent to one thousand prayers (offered elsewhere), so one prayer offered in al-Masjid al-Aqsa is equivalent to two hundred and fifty prayers.

With regard to the well-known hadeeth that says that one prayer offered there is equivalent to five hundred prayers, this hadeeth is da'eef (weak). See Tamaam al-Minnah by Shaykh al-Albaani (may Allaah have mercy on him), p. 292.

Secondly:

A Haram or sanctuary comes under special rulings which were prescribed by Allaah.

For example: it is haraam to fight therein; it is haraam to hunt the animals and birds that live there; it is haraam to cut down the plants that grow there naturally by the will of Allaah and have not been planted by anyone.

Allaah blessed the people of Makkah by making Makkah a sanctuary and safe place for them, in which both people and animals are safe. Allaah says (interpretation of the meaning):

"Have We not established for them a secure sanctuary (Makkah), to which are brought fruits of all kinds, a provision from Ourselves, but most of them know not" [al-Qasas 28:57]

"Have they not seen that We have made (Makkah) a secure sanctuary, while men are being snatched away from all around them?" [al-'Ankaboot 29:67]

"whosoever enters it, he attains security" [Aal 'Imraan 3:97]

Muslim (1362) narrated that Jaabir said: The Prophet (peace and blessings of Allaah be upon him) said: "Ibraaheem made Makkah a sanctuary, and I have made Madeenah a sanctuary…its branches are not to be cut and its animals are not to be hunted."

The word that is translated as "branches" here refers to every kind of tree that has thorns. If it is haraam to cut down the trees that have thorns then it is more appropriate that those that do not have thorns should not be cut down.

And Muslim (1374) narrated that Abu Sa'eed al-Khudri said: The Prophet (peace and blessings of Allaah be upon him) said: "O Allaah, Ibraaheem made Makkah sacred and made it a sanctuary, and I have made Madeenah a sanctuary…no blood is to be shed therein, no weapon for fighting is to be carried, and no tree is to be struck to make its leaves fall, except to provide food for animals…"

Al-Nawawi said:

This shows that it is permissible to take the leaves of plants to provide food for animals. What is meant here is that taking the leaves is haraam except for this purpose.

Al-Quds (Jerusalem) is not a sanctuary in this sense, according to the consensus of the Muslims. People use this word (Haram or sanctuary) in a very broad sense, to such an extent that they call al-Quds a sanctuary, and the Mosque of Ibraaheem al-Khaleel in Palestine a sanctuary, and even universities are called sanctuaries. There are no sanctuaries on earth apart from those in Makkah and Madeenah, and a valley in al-Taa'if called Wujj concerning which the scholars differed as to whether it was a sanctuary or not.

Shaykh al-Islam Ibn Taymiyah said in Majmoo' al-Fataawa, 27/14-15:

Bayt al-Maqdis is not a place that can be called a sanctuary (haram), nor is the Tomb of al-Khaleel or any other place on earth, except for three:

The first is a sanctuary according to the consensus of the Muslims. This is the sanctuary of Makkah, which Allaah has honoured.

The second is a sanctuary according to the majority of scholars. This is the sanctuary of the Prophet (i.e., in Madeenah). This is a sanctuary according to the majority of scholars such as Maalik, al-Shaafa'i and Ahmad. There are many saheeh hadeeth concerning this narrated from the Prophet (peace and blessings of Allaah be upon him).

The third is Wujj, which is a valley in al-Taa'if. There is a hadeeth concerning this that was narrated by Ahmad in al-Musnad, not in the books of Saheeh. This is a sanctuary according to al-Shaafa'i because he believed the hadeeth to be saheeh, but it is not a sanctuary according to the majority of scholars. Ahmad classed as da'eef (weak) the hadeeth that was narrated concerning this and did not accept it.

Places other than these are not sanctuaries according to any of the Muslim scholars. The sanctuary is that in which Allaah has forbidden hunting and cutting its plants, and Allaah has not forbidden hunting and cutting plants in any places except these three.

And Allaah knows best.

Islam Q&A

Appendix L
Changing of the Qibla[119]

(Authors' note: This is a typical smokescreen Islamic response that hides some key facts to represent what appears to be a coherent position.)

Question: as-salaam-u-alikum. I would like to know why Muslims once prayed towards bait-ul-muqadis and why was this changed to the ka'baa. jazakallah

Response by Sheikh Muhammed Salih Al-Munajjid under the title: Why was the Qiblah changed from Bayt al-Maqdis (Jerusalem) to the Ka'bah (Makkah)?

Praise be to Allaah.

When the Prophet (peace and blessings of Allaah be upon him) came from Makkah to Madeenah, he used to face Bayt al-Maqdis when he prayed, and that remained the case for sixteen or seventeen months, as is proven in the two Saheehs (al-Bukhaari and Muslim), in the hadeeth of al-Baraa' ibn 'Aazib (may Allaah be pleased with him and his father), who said: "The Prophet (peace and blessings of Allaah be upon him) prayed towards Bayt al-Maqdis for sixteen or seventeen months, and he was hoping that the Qiblah would be towards the House (i.e., the Ka'bah)..."

Then after that Allaah commanded him to face the direction of the Ka'bah (the Sacred House), in the aayah (interpretation of the meaning): "...so turn your face in the direction of al-Masjid al-Haraam (at Makkah). And wheresoever you people are, turn your faces (in prayer) in that direction..." [al-Baqarah 2:144].

---

[119] http://islamqa.com/en/ref/1953/bayt%20al%20maqdis

Before we answer the question about the wisdom behind this change, we must note the following points:

When we Muslims hear of a command from Allaah, we must accept it and submit to it, even if the wisdom behind it is not clear to us, as Allaah says (interpretation of the meaning): "It is not for a believer, man or woman, when Allaah and His Messenger have decreed a matter, that they should have any option in their decision…" [al-Ahzaab 33:36]

Allaah, may He be glorified and exalted, does not give any command without there being great wisdom behind it – even if we do not understand it – as He says (interpretation of the meaning): "…That is the judgement of Allaah. He judges between you. And Allaah is All-Knowing, All-Wise." [al-Mumtahinah 60:10]

Allaah, may He be glorified and exalted, does not abrogate any rule except to replace it with something better or similar to it, as He says (interpretation of the meaning): "Whatever Verse (revelation) do We abrogate or cause to be forgotten, We bring a better one or similar to it. Know you not that Allaah is able to do all things?" [al-Baqarah 2:106]

Having understood this, we may note that the wisdom behind the changing of the Qiblah has several aspects, including:

It is a test for the true believer, because the true believer, unlike others, accepts the commands of Allaah. Allaah has spoken of this in the Qur'aan (interpretation of the meaning): "…And We made the Qiblah which you used to face, only to test those who followed the Messenger from those who would turn on their heels. Indeed it was great (heavy) except for those whom Allaah guided…" [al-Baqarah 2:143]

This ummah is the best of nations, as Allaah says (interpretation of the meaning): "You are the best of peoples ever raised up for mankind…" [Aal 'Imraan 3:110]. Confirming the aayat about the Qiblah, Allaah says (interpretation of the meaning): "Thus We have made of you (true Muslims) a Wasat (just) (and the best) nation…" [al-Baqarah 2:143]. "Wasat" conveys meanings of justice and of being chosen. So Allaah has chosen for this ummah goodness in all things and the best commands and rules, and thus He chose for them the Qiblah of Ibraaheem, upon whom be peace.

Imaam Ahmad reported in his Musnad (6/134-135) from 'Aa'ishah that the Prophet (peace and blessings of Allaah be upon him) said about the People of the Book (Jews and Christians): "They do not envy us for anything as much as they envy us for Yawm al-Jumu'ah (Friday), to which Allaah has guided us and from which they have gone astray, and for the Qiblah to which Allaah has guided us and from which they have gone astray, and for our saying 'Aameen' behind the imaam." (For more information on this subject, please refer to Bada'i' al-Fawaa'id by Ibn al-Qayyim, may Allaah have mercy on him, 4/157-174).

And Allaah knows best.

Islam Q&A
Sheikh Muhammed Salih Al-Munajjid

Appendix M
The Medina Pact
(In Arabic and English)

1 Arabic Text of the Medina Pact (or Charter)according to Ibn Ishaq (Muhammad's Biographer in the 9th Century)

قال ابن إسحاق : وكتب رسول الله صلى الله عليه وسلم كتابا بين المهاجرين والأنصار ، وادع فيه يهود وعاهدهم وأقرهم على دينهم وأموالهم وشرط لهم واشترط عليهم ﴿بسم الله الرحمن الرحيم هذا كتاب من محمد النبي صلى الله عليه وسلم بين المؤمنين والمسلمين من قريش ويثرب ، ومن تبعهم فلحق بهم وجاهد معهم إنهم أمة واحدة من دون الناس المهاجرون من قريش على ربعتهم يتعاقلون بينهم وهم يفدون عانيهم بالمعروف والقسط بين المؤمنين وبنو عوف على ربعتهم يتعاقلون معاقلهم الأولى ، كل طائفة تفدي عانيها بالمعروف والقسط بين المؤمنين وبنو ساعدة على ربعتهم يتعاقلون معاقلهم الأولى ، وكل طائفة منهم نفدي عانيها بالمعروف والقسط بين المؤمنين وبنو الحارث على ربعتهم يتعاقلون معاقلهم الأولى ، وكل طائفة تفدي عانيها بالمعروف والقسط بين المؤمنين وبنو جشم على ربعتهم يتعاقلون معاقلهم الأولى ، وكل طائفة منهم تفدي عانيها بالمعروف والقسط بين المؤمنين وبنو النجار على ربعتهم يتعاقلون معاقلهم الأولى ، وكل طائفة منهم تفدي عانيها بالمعروف والقسط بين المؤمنين وبنو عمرو بن عوف على ربعتهم يتعاقلون معاقلهم الأولى ، وكل طائفة تفدي عانيها بالمعروف والقسط بين المؤمنين وبنو النبيت على ربعتهم يتعاقلون معاقلهم الأولى ، وكل طائفة تفدي عانيها بالمعروف والقسط بين المؤمنين وبنو الأوس على ربعتهم يتعاقلون معاقلهم الأولى ، وكل طائفة منهم تفدي عانيها بالمعروف والقسط بين المؤمنين وإن المؤمنين لا يتركون مفرحا بينهم أن يعطوه بالمعروف في فداء أو عقل ﴾ .

قال ابن هشام : المفرح المثقل بالدين والكثير العيال . قال الشاعر

وتحمل أخرى أفرحتك الودائع   إذا أنت لم تبرح تؤدي أمانة

وأن لا يحالف مؤمن مولى مؤمن دونه وأن المؤمنين المتقين على من بغى منهم أو ابتغى دسيعة ظلم أو إثم أو عدوان ، أو فساد بين المؤمنين وأن أيديهم عليه جميعا ، ولو كان ولد أحدهم ولا يقتل مؤمن مؤمنا في كافر ولا ينصر كافرا على مؤمن وإن ذمة الله واحدة يجير عليهم أدناهم وإن المؤمنين بعضهم موالي بعض دون الناس وإنه من تبعنا من يهود فإن له النصر والأسوة غير مظلومين ولا متناصرين عليهم وإن سلم المؤمنين واحدة لا يسالم مؤمن دون مؤمن في قتال . في سبيل الله إلا على سواء وعدل بينهم وإن كل غازية غزت معنا يعقب بعضها بعضا ، وإن المؤمنين يبيء بعضهم على بعض بما نال دماءهم في سبيل الله وإن المؤمنين المتقين على أحسن هدي وأقومه وإنه لا يجير مشرك مالا لقريش ولا نفسا ، ولا يحول دونه على مؤمن وإنه من اعتبط مؤمنا قتلا عن بينة فإنه قود به إلا أن يرضى ولي المقتول وإن المؤمنين عليه كافة ولا يحل لهم إلا قيام عليه وإنه لا يحل لمؤمن أقر بما في هذه الصحيفة وآمن بالله واليوم الآخر أن ينصر محدثا ، ولا يؤويه وأنه من نصره أو آواه فإن عليه لعنة الله وغضبه يوم القيامة ولا يؤخذ منه صرف ولا عدل وإنكم مهما اختلفتم فيه من شيء فإن مرده إلى الله عز وجل وإلى محمد صلى الله عليه وسلم وإن اليهود ينفقون مع المؤمنين ما داموا محاربين وإن يهود بني عوف أمة مع المؤمنين لليهود دينهم وللمسلمين دينهم مواليهم وأنفسهم إلا من ظلم وأثم فإنه لا يوتغ إلا نفسه وأهل بيته وإن ليهود بني النجار مثل ما ليهود بني عوف وإن ليهود بني الحارث مثل ما ليهود بني عوف وإن ليهود بني ساعدة مثل ما ليهود بني عوف وإن ليهود بني جشم مثل ما ليهود بني عوف وإن ليهود بني الأوس مثل ما ليهود بني عوف وإن ليهود بني ثعلبة مثل ما ليهود بني عوف إلا من ظلم وأثم فإنه لا يوتغ إلا نفسه وأهل بيته وإن جفنة بطن من ثعلبة كأنفسهم وإن لبني الشطيبة مثل ما ليهود بني عوف وإن البر دون الإثم وإن موالي ثعلبة كأنفسهم وإن بطانة يهود كأنفسهم وإنه لا يخرج منهم أحد إلا بإذن محمد صلى الله عليه وسلم وإنه لا ينحجز على ثأر جرح وإنه من فتك فبنفسه فتك وأهل بيته إلا من ظلم وإن الله على أبر هذا ، وإن على اليهود نفقتهم وعلى المسلمين نفقتهم وإن بينهم النصر على من حارب أهل هذه الصحيفة وإن بينهم النصح والنصيحة والبر دون الإثم وإنه لم يأثم امرئ بحليفه وإن النصر للمظلوم وإن اليهود ينفقون مع المؤمنين ما داموا محاربين وإن يثرب حرام جوفها لأهل هذه الصحيفة وإن الجار كالنفس غير مضار ولا آثم وإنه لا يجار حرمة إلا بإذن أهلها ، وإنه ما كان بين أهل هذه الصحيفة من حدث أو اشتجار يخاف فساده فإن مرده إلى الله عز وجل وإلى محمد رسول الله صلى الله عليه وسلم وإن الله على أتقى ما في هذه الصحيفة وأبره وإنه لا تجار قريش ولا من نصرها ، وإن بينهم النصر على من دهم يثرب ، وإذا دعوا إلى صلح يصالحونه ويلبسونه فإنهم يصالحونه ويلبسونه وإنهم إذا دعوا إلى مثل ذلك فإنه لهم على المؤمنين إلا من حارب في الدين على كل أناس حصتهم من جانبهم الذي قبلهم وإن يهود الأوس ، مواليهم وأنفسهم على مثل ما لأهل هذه الصحيفة مع البر المحض من أهل هذه الصحيفة

قال ابن هشام : ويقال مع البر المحسن من أهل هذه الصحيفة . قال ابن إسحاق : وإن البر دون الإثم لا يكسب كاسب إلا على نفسه وإن الله على أصدق ما في هذه الصحيفة وأبره وإنه لا يحول هذا الكتاب دون ظالم وآثم وإنه من خرج آمن ومن قعد آمن بالمدينة إلا من ظلم أو أثم وإن الله جار لمن بر واتقى ، ومحمد رسول الله صلى الله عليه وسلم

2 English text as provided follows. This is NOT an exact translation of the Arabic text given above.[120]

This is a document from Muhammad the Prophet (may Allah bless him and grant him peace), governing relations between the Believers i.e. Muslims of Quraysh and Yathrib and those who followed them and worked hard with them. They form one nation — Ummah.

The Quraysh Mohajireen will continue to pay blood money, according to their present custom.

In case of war with any body they will redeem their prisoners with kindness and justice common among Believers. (Not according to pre-Islamic nations where the rich and the poor were treated differently).

The Bani Awf will decide the blood money, within themselves, according to their existing custom.

In case of war with anybody all parties other than Muslims will redeem their prisoners with kindness and justice according to practice among Believers and not in accordance with pre-Islamic notions.

The Bani Saeeda, the Bani Harith, the Bani Jusham and the Bani Najjar will be governed on the lines of the above (principles).

The Bani Amr, Bani Awf, Bani Al-Nabeet, and Bani Al-Aws will be governed in the same manner.

Believers will not fail to redeem their prisoners they will pay blood money on their behalf. It will be a common responsibility of the Ummah and not of the family of the prisoners to pay blood money.

A Believer will not make the freedman of another Believer as his ally against the wishes of the other Believers.

The Believers, who fear Allah, will oppose the rebellious elements and those that encourage injustice or sin, or enmity or corruption among Believers.

If anyone is guilty of any such act all the Believers will oppose him even if he be the son of any one of them.

---

[120] http://www.constitution.org/cons/medina/macharter.htm

A Believer will not kill another Believer, for the sake of an un-Believer. (i.e. even though the un-Believer is his close relative).

No Believer will help an un-Believer against a Believer.

Protection (when given) in the Name of Allah will be common. The weakest among Believers may give protection (In the Name of Allah) and it will be binding on all Believers.

Believers are all friends to each other to the exclusion of all others.

Those Jews who follow the Believers will be helped and will be treated with equality. (Social, legal and economic equality is promised to all loyal citizens of the State).

No Jew will be wronged for being a Jew.

The enemies of the Jews who follow us will not be helped.

The peace of the Believers (of the State of Madinah) cannot be divided. (it is either peace or war for all. It cannot be that a part of the population is at war with the outsiders and a part is at peace).

No separate peace will be made by anyone in Madinah when Believers are fighting in the Path of Allah.

Conditions of peace and war and the accompanying ease or hardships must be fair and equitable to all citizens alike.

When going out on expeditions a rider must take his fellow member of the Army-share his ride.

The Believers must avenge the blood of one another when fighting in the Path of Allah (This clause was to remind those in front of whom there may be less severe fighting that the cause was common to all. This also meant that although each battle appeared a separate entity it was in fact a part of the War, which affected all Muslims equally).

The Believers (because they fear Allah) are better in showing steadfastness and as a result receive guidance from Allah in this respect. Others must also aspire to come up to the same standard of steadfastness.

No un-Believer will be permitted to take the property of the Quraysh (the enemy) under his protection. Enemy property must be surrendered to the State.

No un-Believer will intervene in favour of a Quraysh, (because the Quraysh having declared war are the enemy).

If any un-believer kills a Believer, without good cause, he shall be killed in return, unless the next of kin are satisfied (as it creates law and order problems and weakens the defence of the State). All Believers shall be against such a wrong-doer. No Believer will be allowed to shelter such a man.

When you differ on anything (regarding this Document) the matter shall be referred to Allah and Muhammad (may Allah bless him and grant him peace).

The Jews will contribute towards the war when fighting alongside the Believers.

The Jews of Bani Awf will be treated as one community with the Believers. The Jews have their religion. This will also apply to their freedmen. The exception will be those who act unjustly and sinfully. By so doing they wrong themselves and their families.

The same applies to Jews of Bani Al-Najjar, Bani Al Harith, Bani Saeeda, Bani Jusham, Bani Al Aws, Thaalba, and the Jaffna, (a clan of the Bani Thaalba) and the Bani Al Shutayba.

Loyalty gives protection against treachery. (loyal people are protected by their friends against treachery. As long as a person remains loyal to the State he is not likely to succumb to the ideas of being treacherous. He protects himself against weakness).

The freedmen of Thaalba will be afforded the same status as Thaalba themselves. This status is for fair dealings and full justice as a right and equal responsibility for military service.

Those in alliance with the Jews will be given the same treatment as the Jews.

No one (no tribe which is party to the Pact) shall go to war except with the permission of Muhammed (may Allah bless him and grant him peace). If any wrong has been done to any person or party it may be avenged.

Any one who kills another without warning (there being no just cause for it) amounts to his slaying himself and his household, unless the killing was done due to a wrong being done to him.

The Jews must bear their own expenses (in War) and the Muslims bear their expenses.

If anyone attacks anyone who is a party to this Pact the other must come to his help.

They (parties to this Pact) must seek mutual advice and consultation.

Loyalty gives protection against treachery. Those who avoid mutual consultation do so because of lack of sincerity and loyalty.

A man will not be made liable for misdeeds of his ally.

Anyone (any individual or party) who is wronged must be helped.

The Jews must pay (for war) with the Muslims. (this clause appears to be for occasions when Jews are not taking part in the war. Clause 37 deals with occasions when they are taking part in war).

Yathrib will be Sanctuary for the people of this Pact.

A stranger (individual) who has been given protection (by anyone party to this Pact) will be treated as his host (who has given him protection) while (he is) doing no harm and is not committing any crime. Those given protection but indulging in anti-state activities will be liable to punishment.

A woman will be given protection only with the consent of her family (Guardian). (a good precaution to avoid inter-tribal conflicts).

In case of any dispute or controversy, which may result in trouble the matter must be referred to Allah and Muhammed (may Allah bless him and grant him peace), The Prophet (may Allah bless him and grant him peace) of Allah will accept anything in this document, which is for (bringing about) piety and goodness.

Quraysh and their allies will not be given protection.

The parties to this Pact are bound to help each other in the event of an attack on Yathrib.

If they (the parties to the Pact other than the Muslims) are called upon to make and maintain peace (within the State) they must do so. If a similar demand (of making and maintaining peace) is made on the Muslims, it must be carried out, except when the Muslims are already engaged in a war in the Path of Allah. (so that no secret ally of the enemy can aid the enemy by calling upon Muslims to end hostilities under this clause).

Everyone (individual) will have his share (of treatment) in accordance with what party he belongs to. Individuals must benefit or suffer for the good or bad deed of the group they belong to. Without such a rule party affiliations and discipline cannot be maintained.

The Jews of al-Aws, including their freedmen, have the same standing, as other parties to the Pact, as long as they are loyal to the Pact. Loyalty is a protection against treachery.

Anyone who acts loyally or otherwise does it for his own good (or loss).

Allah approves this Document.

This document will not (be employed to) protect one who is unjust or commits a crime (against other parties of the Pact).

Whether an individual goes out to fight (in accordance with the terms of this Pact) or remains in his home, he will be safe unless he has committed a crime or is a sinner. (i.e. No one will be punished in his individual capacity for not having gone out to fight in accordance with the terms of this Pact).

Allah is the Protector of the good people and those who fear Allah, and Muhammad (may Allah bless him and grant him peace) is the Messenger of Allah (He guarantees protection for those who are good and fear Allah).